'Pataphysics

'Pataphysics

The Poetics of an
Imaginary Science

CHRISTIAN BÖK

Northwestern

University Press

Evanston,

Illinois

Northwestern University Press
www.nupress.northwestern.edu

Printed in the United States of America

10   9   8   7   6   5   4   3   2

ISBN-13: 978-0-8101-1876-8 (cloth)

ISBN-10: 0-8101-1876-9 (cloth)

ISBN-13: 978-0-8101-1877-5 (paper)

ISBN-10: 0-8101-1877-7 (paper)

Library of Congress Cataloging-in-Publication Data

Bök, Christian, 1966–

'Pataphysics : the poetics of an imaginary science / Christian Bök.

p. cm.

Includes bibliographical references.

ISBN 0-8101-1876-9 (cloth : alk. paper)—

ISBN 0-8101-1877-7 (paper : alk. paper)

1. Philosophy in literature. 2. Literature and science. I. Title.

PN49.B62   2001

809'.93384—dc21

2001001964

∞ The paper used in this publication meets the minimum
requirements of the American National Standard for Information
Sciences—Permanence of Paper for Printed Library Materials,
ANSI Z39.48-1992.

Contents

Acknowledgments

This book would not have been possible without the gracious support of many academic mentors, including Charles Bernstein, Claudio Duran, Ray Ellenwood, Barbara Godard, Kim Maltman, Marjorie Perloff, and Robert Wallace. I also wish to thank friends and family for their encouragement over the years during the writing of this text: George Book, Sandra Book, Stephen Cain, Natalee Caple, Craig Dworkin, Kenneth Goldsmith, Lori Iseman, Carl Johnston, Steve McCaffery, and Darren Wershler-Henry.

’Pataphysics

Prologue

The Museum of Jurassic Technology in Los Angeles is a strange gallery, where incredible verities integrate so perfectly with believable untruths that a visitor may not detect the peculiar slippage from fact to hoax. Wilson, the curator, has rebuilt the *Wunderkammern* of medieval archives, presenting cabinets and vitrines, full of bizarre curiosa — specimens: not only of *Myotis lucifugus* (a bat whose sonar system can be modulated to create apertures through substantive barriers) but of *Megaloponera foetens* (an ant whose nerve system can be controlled by fungal parasites for replicative purposes). Wilson does not simply repeat the grotesque spectacle of Ripley, since the museum does not present the truth of the absurd with the command *Believe it or not!* Instead, the museum presents the truth as itself absurd with the question *What is it to believe or not?*

Weschler observes that "Wilson has . . . pitched his museum at the very intersection of the premodern and the postmodern" (1995, 90), inserting the visitor into the interstice between *wondering-at* and *wondering-whether*— a gap into which this survey wishes to insert its own reader.[1] What Wilson calls "Jurassic technology" we might call "Jarryite 'pataphysics" — a science of imaginary solutions, in which the critic wishes not only to study but also to evoke cases of exceptional singularity. Like Jarry (who willfully occupies an ambiguous interzone between ratiocination and hallucination), Wilson hopes to imbricate the technical truth of modern science with the medieval magic of poetic wisdom. This survey likewise strives to indulge in such a figural project, since it too proposes the potential existence of a heretofore chimerical science.

'Pataphysics represents a supplement to metaphysics, accenting it, then replacing it, in order to create a philosophic alternative to rationalism. What Wilson has performed, Jarry has predicted: the disappearance of scientificity itself when reason is pushed to its own logical extreme. Such a 'pataphysical qualification of rational validity is symptomatic of a postmodern transition in science from absolutism to relativism. When even time itself fades away into spectacular uncertainty, the very idea that a historical technology might be called "Jurassic" no longer seems wholly absurd (since we can now imagine a futuristic apocalypse, in which cloning might allow a human to coexist with a resurrected tyrannosaur — just as cinema has cloned the image of an actual thespian and spliced it with the image of an unreal sauropod).[2]

'Pataphysics is speculative, waiting for its chance to happen, as if by accident, in a theme park of scientific conception. Like the museum of Wilson, this survey on Jarry attempts to scramble the Jurassic sequence of history so that what is extinct in the past can be called forth again out of its context into the present where the idea of the past itself can in turn be made extinct.[3] For 'pataphysics, any science sufficiently retarded in progress must seem magical (but only after the fact), just as any science sufficiently advanced in progress must seem magical (but only before the fact) — and if 'pataphysics is itself thaumaturgic, it is so not because of any ironic nostalgia for a prehistoric past but only because of its oneiric prognosis for an ahistoric future. We see science itself vanish before the zero degree of its own antiscience.

Structured as a descriptive explication, which emphasizes a theoretical perspective, this survey argues that Jarry has provided an often neglected but still important influence upon the poetic legacy of this century (particularly the Italian Futurists, the French Oulipians, and the Canadian Jarryites). While my survey focuses upon theories of textual poetics rather than poetry itself (relying upon the kind of Nietzschean sophistries that have come to characterize the work of such French rebels as Baudrillard, Deleuze, Derrida, Serres, et al.), my survey does nevertheless strive to be as conceptually encyclopedic as 'pataphysics itself: instead of normalizing 'pataphysics within one theoretical perspective, this survey alludes intermittently to 'pataphysical enterprises that constitute exceptions to such a genealogy of Jarryites.

Recounting the transition from 'pataphysics to "pataphysics (from the single apostrophe of France to the double apostrophe of Canada), this survey reflects the influence of Jarry upon my own poetic career (in particular: my 'pataphysical encyclopedia, *Crystallography*). Inspired by the etymology of the word "crystallography," such a work represents an act of *lucid writing*, which uses the language of geological science to misread the poetics of rhetorical language. Such lucid writing does not concern itself with the transparent transmission of a message (so that, ironically, the poetry often seems "opaque");[4] instead, lucid writing concerns itself with the exploratory examination of its own pattern (in a manner reminiscent of *lucid dreaming*). The capricious philosophy of 'pataphysics is itself an oneiric science aware of its own status as a dream.

'Pataphysics reveals that science is not as "lucid" as once thought, since science must often ignore the arbitrary, if not whimsical, status of its own axioms. Like the work of some 'pataphysicians (particularly the Oulipians), who make a spectacle of such epistemic formality by writing texts according to an absurd, but strict, rule of machinic artifice, this survey also expresses its own extreme of nomic rigor (in this case, grammatical parallelism): each sentence develops a chiastic symmetry as balanced as the contrast in physics between *meta* and *pata*. The arbitrary character of such a constraint does not simply constitute a stylistic frivolity but strives 'pataphysically (if not allegorically) to dramatize a scientific perversion: that the universe is itself an arbitrary formality, whose rules have created a science that can in turn discuss such rules.

'Pataphysics valorizes the exception to each rule in order to subvert the procrustean constraints of science. While this survey may do little to change the mind of a customary scientist (who must ignore the 'pataphysical peculiarity of science itself in order to avoid the charge of crackpot delusion), my survey may nevertheless convince poets to qualify their own Luddite attitude toward science. Such poets might recognize that, if poetry cannot oppose science by becoming its antonymic extreme, perhaps poetry can oppose science by becoming its hyperbolic extreme, using reason against itself 'pataphysically in order to subvert not only pedantic theories of noetic truth but also romantic theories of poetic genius. Such poets might learn to embrace the absurd nature of sophistic reasoning in order to dispute the power of both the real and the true.

Vaneigem, however, warns us that, because of this sophistry, "Joe Soap intellectuals, [']pataphysicians . . .—bandwagon after bandwagon works out its own version of the *credo quia absurdum est:* you [do not] believe in it, but you do it anyway" ([1967] 1994, 178) so that, as a result, "[']pataphysics . . . leads us with many a twist and turn to the last graveyards" (126). While such charges of nihilistic conformism do apply to the work of some 'pataphysicians (particularly Sandomir and Shattuck), such misgivings do not take into account that, like Nietzsche, Jarry does radicalize philosophy, lampooning pedagogic authority, in order to foment a spirit of permanent rebellion, be it antibourgeois or antiphilistine.[5] My survey suggests that this apparent strategy of "indifference" in 'pataphysics merely serves to satirize the impartiality of science itself.

'Pataphysics refuses to conform to any academic standard: hence, this survey cannot demonstrate that it has learned the lessons of its topic without also negotiating a virtually untenable ambiguity between the noetic mandate of scholarship and the poetic license of 'pataphysics. Since no literary history has ever traced in detail the unorthodox genealogy of this avant-garde pseudoscience, I hope that my survey might offer a *Wunder-*

kammern of literary teratism, cataloging the scientific exceptions to the given norms of poetry in order to create an absurd museum of "Jurassic" machines. Just as the anachronism of an iron tool from before the Ice Age might disrupt our sense of temporal security, so also might such an archive of anomaly recontextualize the given canon of modern poetry. Let us imagine a future for such an impossible philosophy.

Non cum vacaveris, pataphysicandum est.
   —Jarry [1944] 1965, 39

[T]he encyclopaedia said: For one of these gnostics, the visible
universe was an illusion or (more precisely) a sophism.
   —Borges [1962] 1983, 8

The debt that [']pataphysics owes to sophism cannot be overstated.
   —Bernstein 1994, 105

1. Science and Poetry
The Differend of the *Ur* in 'Pataphysics

Quasi Realities

Borges in *Tlön, Uqbar, Orbis Tertius* imagines an allegory about the
seductions of simulation. A secret cabal of rebel artists has conspired to
replace the actual world, piece by piece, with a virtual world, so that the
inertia of a true history vanishes, phase by phase, into the amnesia of a
false memory. The irony is that this conspiracy meets with no resistance:
"[a]lmost immediately, reality yielded on more than one account" for "[t]he
truth is that it longed to yield" ([1956] 1983, 22)—to disappear into its own
phantasms. All things embrace the weirdness of this astonishing event and
ignore the piousness of all admonishing truth. The event foments a revolution in philosophy—a shift away from the nomic study of what is veritable
to a ludic study of what is possible, as if "every philosophy is by definition
a dialectical game, a *Philosophie des Als Ob*" (14).

Borges imagines a reality where to imagine a reality can cause a reality
to exist ex nihilo. Each memory of an object conjures the miracle of a *hrön*,
the replica of a replica; and yet, "[s]tranger and more pure than any *hrön*
is, at times, the *ur*" (an ectype without prototype), "the object produced
through suggestion, educed by hope" ([1956] 1983, 18).[1] Like the *tlönistas*
who believe that "metaphysics is a branch of fantastic literature" (14), the
narrator of this fantasy pretends to believe in such an imaginary philosophy,
quoting fictitious references to it in gazettes and treatises. His alternative

7

to metaphysics is itself an *ur* because his dream of it has indeed come true, not only in his story but also in our world. We too fulfill this apocalyptic conspiracy by creating, for ourselves, a world where fantasy has more reality than reality itself.

Postmodernism in fact defines itself in terms of such a catastrophe. Philosophy has everywhere begun to threaten the constraints of both the real and the true in order to practice an antiphilosophy—what Jarry might call by the name of *'pataphysics,* the science of imaginary solutions and arbitrary exceptions ([1911] 1965, 192). Jarry suggests through 'pataphysics that reality does not exist, except as the interpretive projection of a phenomenal perspective—which is to say that reality is never *as it is* but always *as if it is.* Reality is quasi, pseudo: it is more virtual than actual; it is real only to the degree to which it can seem to be real and only for so long as it can be made to stay real. Science for such a reality has increasingly become what Vaihinger might call a "philosophy of *as if* " (1966, xvii), willfully mistaking possibilities for veritabilities.

Baudrillard observes that, for the "[']Pataphysics of the year 2000," history has accelerated past the escape velocity for reality, moving from the centrifugal gravity of the real into the centripetal celerity of the void" ([1992] 1994a, 1). Events occur in the null-space of simulation, where "[a]ll metaphysical tension has been dissipated, yielding a [']pataphysical ambiance" ([1983] 1990a, 71). Things succumb to relativity, complexity, and uncertainty, shifting from an absolute state of determinism to a dissolute field of indeterminism. The science of 'pataphysics responds to these absurdities with a genre of science fiction that shows science itself to be a fiction. It narrates not *what is,* but *what might have become.* It inhabits the tense of the future perfect, of the *post modo*—a paradoxical temporality, in which what has yet to happen has already taken place.

The *Ur* of Science

Jarry claims that 'pataphysics studies "the universe supplementary to this one," but not simply an adjunct reality so much as an ersatz reality, "a universe which can be . . . envisaged in the place of the traditional one" ([1911] 1965, 131). Such a supplement is always more substitutive than augmentative, replacing reality instead of accenting reality—and ironically, the science that studies such a supplement is itself a supplement. It is "the science of that which is superinduced upon metaphysics" as both an excess and a redress, "extending as far beyond metaphysics as the latter extends beyond physics" (131). An auxiliary substitute that compensates for a lack in philosophy even as it impregnates the form of philosophy, such a science simulates knowledge, perpetrating a hoax, really and truly, but only to reveal the hoax of both the real and the true.

Jarry performs humorously on behalf of literature what Nietzsche performs seriously on behalf of philosophy. Both thinkers in effect attempt to dream up a "gay science," whose joie de vivre thrives wherever the tyranny of truth has increased our esteem for the lie and wherever the tyranny of reason has increased our esteem for the mad. Both thinkers lay the groundwork for an antiphilosophy, whose spirit of reform has come to characterize such alternatives to metaphysics as the grammatology of Derrida, the schizanalysis of Deleuze, or the homeorrhetics of Serres. All such antimetaphysical metaphilosophies argue that anomalies extrinsic to a system remain secretly intrinsic to such a system. The most credible of truths always evolves from the most incredible of errors. The praxis of science always involves the parapraxis of poetry.

'Pataphysics, "the science of the particular" (Jarry [1911] 1965, 131), does not, therefore, study the rules governing the general recurrence of a periodic incident (the *expected* case) so much as study the games governing the special occurrence of a sporadic accident (the *excepted* case). 'Pataphysics not only studies exception but has itself become an exception—dismissed and neglected despite its influence and relevance. Jarry has not only inspired the absurdity of nearly every modern avant-garde but has also predicted the absurdity of nearly all modern technoscience. No history, however, has ever traced in detail this unorthodox genealogy, even though contemporary philosophy has begun to shift its emphasis from the metaphysical to the antimetaphysical—a trend that only a few critics (e.g., Dufresne and McCaffery) have dared to describe as 'pataphysical in nature.

'Pataphysics has ultimately determined the horizon of thought for any encounter between philosophy and literature, but criticism has largely ignored this important principle of the postmodern condition. What irony: 'pataphysics has replaced metaphysics so slowly and subtly that, once noticed, the transition seems at once sudden and abrupt. This survey therefore intends to redress the surprise of such amnesia by revising the history of both science and poetry in order to bring 'pataphysics to bear upon 'pataphysics itself. Such revision, of course, faces obstacles, not the least of which is the fact that 'pataphysics is imaginary. No such discipline exists. What then is there to study? What museums can house its relics? What codexes can record its axioms? Such a science may be no more than an *ur*—a last hope that has yet to come true.

'Pataphysics does not pretend to unify its parts into a system or to ratify its ploys into an agenda. Such a casual science has no theory, no method (even though Jarry has since inspired writers to create the College of 'Pataphysics, aspects of which allude to a fictional archive, the Grand Academy of Lagado). Such a casual science also has no manual, no primer (even though Jarry has since inspired critics to study the Elements of 'Pataphysics, excerpts of which appear in a fictional almanac, a Treatise by Doctor Faustroll). Like the abridged treatise on Tlön, the incomplete handbook of Jarry compels its readers to finish the job of converting the fake image of a virtual science into a real thing in the actual universe. Even this survey may not explain the existence of 'pataphysics so much as conjure 'pataphysics into existence.

Jarry implies that such a science can be written only with an invisible ink, "sulphate of quinine," whose words remain unseen until read in the dark under the "infrared rays of a spectrum whose other colors [are] locked in an opaque box" ([1911] 1965, 191–92). Such a science cannot be seen except under a light that cannot be seen in a place that cannot be seen. Such a science exists paradoxically in an eigenstate of indeterminate potentiality, not unlike the Schrödinger cat—both there and not there at the same time. Not philosophy, but philosophastry, such a science at first appears scandalous and superfluous because it delights in the eclectic and the esoteric. It encourages a promiscuous economy of indiscriminate exchanges, playfully conjugating paradoxes in order to make possible an absolute expenditure of thought without any absolute investiture in thought.

'Pataphysics thus heralds apocalyptically what Baudrillard calls a "casual form of writing to match the casual *événementialité* of our age"—a spiraling commentary upon "*the Grande Gidouille* of History" ([1992], 1994a, 17). This survey attempts to practice such a writing of history in the belief that theory must explore as much as it must explain. To do otherwise is to reduce the science of 'pataphysics to another species of hermeneutics: just a way to read, not a way to live. To write against metaphysics, with its good sense and its good taste, is not to shirk the duties of the critic but to wager their values against the demand for change. If we are to take 'pataphysics seriously, are we not obliged to be exceptional? If this survey threatens to meander, is this not because it imitates the vortices of a *gidouille* in order to maintain an element of surprise?

Surprise breaks the promise of the expected: it is the exception that disturbs the suspense of what we know must happen next. Hence, this survey offers the following itinerary about things to come in the hope that we might later be surprised by the unexpected. This survey begins by tracing the history of the conflict between science and poetry in order to contextualize 'pataphysics within the four phases of such dispute (the *animatismic*, the *mechanismic*, the *organismic*, and the *cyborganismic*). The survey then discusses 'pataphysics itself, defining three declensions of exception (the *anomalos*, the *syzygia*, and the *clinamen*), doing so not only to show the diverse parallels between the work of Jarry and Nietzsche but also to relate such work to the diverse projects of such contemporary philosophers as Baudrillard, Derrida, Deleuze, and Serres.

Subsequently, the survey traces the influence of Jarry on three cases of avant-garde pseudoscience (the Italian Futurists, the French Oulipians, and the Canadian Jarryites). Each movement revises a prior schema about the structure of exception in order to disrupt the normalization of the 'pataphysical: for the Futurists, exception results from the collision of machines; for the Oulipians, exception results from the constraint of programs; and for the Jarryites, exception results from the corruption of memories. Like these movements, this survey also tries to avoid the normalization of the 'pataphysical, doing so by alluding intermittently to 'pataphysical enterprises that do not refer to the tradition of Jarry but nevertheless represent some of the exceptions to the genealogy that this survey posits.

Exceptions, after all, can resort to an assortment of modalities: variance (*anomalos*), alliance (*syzygia*), or deviance (*clinamen*). The *anomalos* finds a way to differ from every other thing in a system that values the norm of equivalence; the *syzygia* finds a way to equate things to each other in a system that values the norm of difference; and the *clinamen* finds a way to detour around things in a system that values the fate of contrivance. All three modes of exception do inform this survey on 'pataphysics so that, if its style risks everything to disrupt, to confuse, and to digress, it does so not for any lack of formal rigor but for the sake of a crucial thesis. Can a ludic theory of 'pataphysics be fairly judged by the nomic values of metaphysics if 'pataphysics criticizes metaphysics itself? Are we not obliged to consider the problem of this question?

'Pataphysics, strangely enough, has two parallel histories that act out opposite strategies for criticizing such a scientific metaphysics: first, the irrationalism of the Symbolists, the Dadaists, and the Surrealists (all of whom argue for a poetic emancipation from science); second, the surrationalism of the Futurists, the Oulipians, and the Jarryites (all of whom argue for a poetic appropriation of science). Jarry has influenced both strategies despite their opposition. The Futurists attack the Symbolists, for example, just as the Oulipians attack the Surrealists. Both cases of conflict pit the pragmatic formalism of postmodernity against the aesthetic mysticism of modernity. What is at stake is the status of poetry in a world of science. How might poetry reclaim its own viable truth? How might science benefit from its own poetic irony?

Surrationalism, for example, responds to such questions not only by using the forms of poetry to criticize the myths of science (its pedantic theories of expressive truth) but also by using the forms of science to criticize the myths of poetry (its romantic theories of expressive genius). Surrationalism has accented this conflict between science and poetry in three different ways. The Futurists inflect the machinic intensities of technological forms; the Oulipians inflect the mathetic intensities of numerological forms; and the Jarryites inflect the mnemonic intensities of paleological forms. This survey focuses largely upon these three surrational movements not only because they have better expressed the original intentions of 'pataphysics, but also because they have received less critical attention from theoreticians.

Surrationalism is thus just as exceptional as it is 'pataphysical, defining a regime for the avant-garde, not only in poetry but also in science. Bachelard suggests that all scientific radicalism begins with "an *époche,* a placing of reality between parentheses" ([1940] 1968, 28) so that science might systematically explore an otherwise impossible hypothesis: "it is in this area of dialectical surrationalism that the scientific mind *dreams*" (32). Every question about *what if* leads to a science of *as if.* No longer limited by one case of nature, science can propose many modes of reason: for example, the non-Euclidean geometry of Riemann or the non-Boolean algebra of Korzybski. We see science interrogate itself in order to relativize itself. It can no longer take its reality for granted but must account for its history: the reason of its reason.

Baudrillard suggests that, while metaphysics is the *anti* of simulation (opposing fantasy with ever more reality), 'pataphysics is the *ante* of simulation (opposing fantasy with ever more fantasy): "only a [']*pataphysics of simulacra* can remove us from the . . . strategy of simulation and the impasse of death in which it imprisons us," and "[t]his supreme ruse of the system . . . , only a superior ruse can stop" ([1981] 1994b, 153–54). Metaphysics is a supreme ruse because it makes us believe in the true; 'pataphysics is a superior ruse because it lets us pretend to be untrue. Truth implodes upon itself and reveals an aporia at its center—the "[d]ead point . . . where every system crosses this subtle limit of . . . contradiction . . . and enters live into non-contradiction"—the ecstasy of thought: "[h]ere begins a [']pataphysics of systems" ([1983] 1990a, 14).

The *Ur* of History

Beginnings: let us digress for a moment; let us begin with a swerve. Ubu, the "Professor of [']pataphysics," steps on stage at the turn of the century in order to announce "a branch of science which we have invented and for which a crying need is generally experienced" (Jarry [1944] 1965, 26–27). An imaginary science thus makes its debut in a millenary instant, appearing at the transition from a romantic era to a modernist era, when metaphysics has totalized, but not yet optimized, its power to speak the truth. If poetry has failed to oppose science by being its antonymic extreme, then perhaps poetry can attempt to oppose science by being its hyperbolic extreme. An absurd science that might dissect contradictions has itself enacted contradictions. It has simultaneously affirmed and negated not only its belief in but also its doubts about the values of reason.

Science has historically legitimated itself by practicing a *contemptus historia*. Theories in the past that differ from theories in the present must forfeit their validity. History becomes nothing more than what Canguilhem might call *le passé dépassé* ([1989] 1994, 27), a museum of error, where time can cause any concept to become as quaint as a metaphor.[2] Whenever science deigns to think its history, it narrates a transition from the falsity of poetry to the verity of science, even though history sees science not as the progress to truth but as the congress of truth—a quorum of dispute, where the right to speak the truth is itself at stake. The surrationalism of 'pataphysics might pursue this line of reasoning in order to suggest that in fact science replaces its errors not with other errata but with other errors, each one more subtle than the last one.

Science errs when it sees its history as a consecutive process of both accumulation and amelioration. When tracing the history of the term "physical," from the discourse of Aristotle (*physikos*), through the discourse of Bacon (*physica*), to the discourse of Heisenberg (*physics*), science often presumes not only that each discourse is the nascent form of the next discourse but also that each discourse is a variant form of the same discourse: *scientia*. The word "science," however, does not designate the coherent progress of one rational practice but instead signifies an unstable array of logical tactics whose local, synergistic conflict can invoke, provoke, and revoke a global, syllogistic program: *deduction* through dialectics (for Aristotle); *induction* through empiricism (for Bacon); and *abduction* through statistics (for Heisenberg).

'Pataphysics reveals that, like poetry, science has an avant-garde with its own history of dissent. What Deleuze and Guattari might call the *royal sciences* of efficient productivity have historically repressed and exploited the *nomad sciences* of expedient adaptability ([1980] 1987, 362). A royal science is a standardized metaphysics: it is deployed by the state throughout a clathrate, Cartesian space, putting truth *to work* on behalf of solid, instrumental imperatives (law and order). A nomad science is a bastardized metaphysics: it is deployed against the state throughout an aggregate, Riemannian space, putting truth *at risk* on behalf of fluid, experimental operatives (trial and error). Such scientific economies are contrastive but not exclusive. They transect at many points across many scales, each one immanent in the other, like a postponed potential.

Royal sciences value the renovation of what Kuhn calls a "paradigm" (1970, 10), a nomic language-game that must systematically (im)prove its own consistency and efficiency by *solving* problems, *revoking* anomaly for the sake of what is normal and known.[3] Nomad sciences, however, value the innovation of what Lyotard calls a "paralogy" ([1979] 1984, 60), a ludic language-game that must systematically (ap)prove its own inconsistency and inefficiency by *convolving* problems, *invoking* anomaly for the sake of what is abnormal and unknown. These two economies do not oppose each other so much as enfold each other. They inflect opposite values of intent within a composite system of truth. A failure in one language-game played according to one set of rules always determines the rules of success for a new language-game played according to a new set of rules.

'Pataphysics no doubt defines the rubric for this kind of nomadic paralogy. Itinerant and sophistic, all such surrationalism reveals that science, like poetry, changes only when it deploys what Shklovsky might call a tactic of *ostranenie,* of estrangement ([1917] 1965, 12). Scientific revolutions may be nothing more than metaphoric revolutions, in which autotelic novelties foreground the dramatization of a system in order to undermine the automatization of its reason. Paradigm shifts reveal that every axiology secretly involves a reductio ad absurdum—the anomaly of an irresistible, but inadmissible, theorem. The aporia of such a system arises paradoxically from the rigor of its logic—as if its success also means its failure. The sudden triumph of 'pataphysics thus does not imply the utter defeat of metaphysics so much as the pyrrhic victory of metaphysics.

Lyotard observes that, because science creates a method by which to correct the errors that it detects in its method, science is "a process of delegitimation fueled by the demand for legitimation itself" ([1979] 1984, 39). Interdiction by a paradigm against contradiction in the paradigm causes the paradigm to exclude, as extrinsic from it, a paralogy intrinsic to it: "science—by concerning itself with such things as undecidables . . . is theorizing its own evolution as . . . paradoxical" (60). Ironically, the system that yearns to validate itself only learns to invalidate itself. No longer does science rationalize its truth so much as relativize its truth. We adopt "a model of legitimation that has nothing to do with maximized performance" (60) but rather implies "a model of an 'open system,' in which a statement becomes relevant if it 'generates ideas'" (64).

Science graphs a rhizomatic flowchart of stratified trajectories, an agonistic force field of diversified catastrophes, some of which collide with each other, some of which collude with each other, all of which operate together simultaneously in fits and starts at asynchronous rates of incommensurate change. Science is a complex tissue of hybrid tensions, its metaphors not only reflecting each other but also refracting each other. They facilitate changes to an economy of exchanges by accentuating all the unforeseen instabilities in scientific signification. Like poetry, science is a bricolage of figures, an assemblage of devices, none of which fit together perfectly— but unlike poetry, science must nevertheless subject its tropes to a system, whose imperatives of both verity and reality normally forbid any willing suspension of disbelief.

Science and poetry have shared a common history, undergoing four phases of distinct change (the *animatismic,* the *mechanismic,* the *organismic,* and the *cyborganismic*); nevertheless, the two disciplines have not evolved in tandem or in sync. Foucault observes, for example, that science and poetry have evolved opposite relations to the authorial function ([1969] 1977, 125–26). Science moves toward anonymity. Poetry moves toward eponymity. The absence of the author in science serves an *allotelic* interest (justifying itself for the sake of a finality outside its own language), while the presence of the author in poetry serves an *autotelic* interest (justifying itself for the sake of a finality inside its own language). Whenever science gains the anonymous power to speak the truth about things, poetry seeks an eponymous refuge in the space of its own words.

Allotelic interests have always regarded autotelic interests as a waste of time, particularly in a capitalist economy where only the most effective arsenal of productive tactics can prevail. Is it any wonder then that, for such imperial cynicism, science and poetry function within a relation not of genre but of power? The waxing influence of science has always implied the waning relevance of poetry—as if science must capitalize upon the competition for truth in order to monopolize the legitimation of truth. The science of 'pataphysics, however, expresses on behalf of poetry what the metaphysics of science represses in itself: its own basis in signs, their errors and biases—the ideology of metaphor. The autotelic aspect of science (its ludic surrationalism) always threatens to radicalize the allotelic agenda of science (its nomic rationalism).

Althusser argues that, although ideology always involves a *denegation* of itself so that subjects produced by it cannot recognize themselves within it, the allotelic anonymity of science means that the clarity of its language can nevertheless negate ideology, yet successfully remain impartial: "ideology *has no outside* (for itself), but at the same time . . . *it is nothing but outside* (for science . . .)" ([1970] 1971, 175). Barthes disagrees, however, arguing that science is never neutral. Instead, science interpellates its subject as an absence—a vanishing point, projected within ideology as though beyond ideology: "the scholar excludes himself in a concern for objectivity; yet what is excluded is never anything but the 'person' . . . , not the subject; moreover, this subject is filled . . . with the very exclusion it . . . imposes upon its person" ([1984] 1986, 8).

Barthes suggests that science differs from poetry not because of any disparity between them in format, content, method, or intent but because of a disparity between them in status—a prestige of pedagogy ([1984] 1986, 3). Whereas poetry has always offered an egalitarian regime, destabilizing the *signifier* within a generalized economy of polysemic enunciation, science has only offered a totalitarian regime, stabilizing the *signified* within a restricted economy of monosemic enunciation. For Barthes, science must begin to acknowledge its ideological investments, radicalizing itself by poeticizing itself. If ideology is the unreal conciliation of a real contradiction, is it not fair to say that ideology is itself an imaginary solution—and therefore 'pataphysical? If metaphysics must study the ontology of truth, must not 'pataphysics study the ideology of power?

Ultimately, the conflict between science and poetry concerns this power to speak the truth, and this power has undergone four phases of epistemic transition: the *animatismic* phase, whose truth involves interpreting signs through an act of *exegesis;* the *mechanismic* phase, whose truth involves disquisiting signs through an act of *mathesis;* the *organismic* phase, whose truth involves implementing signs through an act of *anamnesis;* and the *cyborganismic* phase, whose truth involves deregulating signs through an act of *catamnesis.* The life sciences, for example, have progressed from the *biomagy* of animatism, through the *biotaxy* of mechanism, through the *biology* of organism, to the *bionics* of cyborganism. Each phase involves not only a different definition of science and poetry but also a different opposition between them.

During the animatismic phase, when papal academies divide discourse scholastically into modes of textualization and numeralization (*trivium* and *quadrivium*), knowledge is rarefied largely because of its insufficient supply. During the mechanismic phase, when royal academies divide discourse aristocratically into modes of investigation and dissemination, knowledge is rarefied largely because of its unspecialized market. During the organismic phase, when state academies divide discourse democratically into modes of ratiocination and acculturation (*scientia* and *humanitas*), knowledge is rarefied because of its specialized labor. And during the cyborganismic phase, when state academies divide discourse plutocratically into modes of totalization and optimization, knowledge is rarefied largely because of its overabundant supply.

The Animatismic Phase

Foucault observes that, before empiricism, "*divinatio* and *eruditio* are both part of the same hermeneutics" ([1969] 1973, 34). Medieval treatises on natural history establish no criterion for the condition of relevance, since such treatises merely compile *legenda,* collecting together haphazardly all the random lore about a sample topic in order to document the complex heraldry of its textual spectrum: "none of these forms of discourse is required to justify its claim to be expressing a truth before it is interpreted; all that is required of it is the possibility of talking about it" (40). Science in its animatismic phase sees that signs exist long before being known: they are written into things by nature, and they extinguish the distance between things in order to reveal the synchronic continuum of their secret order.

Reality for the animatismic phase is a stable orrery that revolves around a central fulcrum. Knowing such a reality involves an exegetic function, reading signs, interpreting them, rearranging them within an anagram that permutes all their modes of sympathy and antipathy. Such an anatomy of forms distributes signs aesthetically throughout a nomad regime in which all things must conform to an order of both resemblance and concordance. Even the difference between the reasoning of science and the imagining of poetry does not yet exist because no paradigm provides a consensus for such verities. Each text has equal truthfulness. Each myth can convey what Vico might call a "poetic wisdom" ([1744] 1984, 110), whose truth owes its power to an error that demands belief in a "credible impossibility" (120)— an *as if* that can provide the premise in the future for a *scienza nuova*.[4]

Poetic wisdom simply monopolizes the totality of both the subject and the object, leaving no space for modern science to speak the truth for itself except as an act of deviance within such a norm. Poetic wisdom cannot recognize any disparity between the subjective affect of imagining and the objective effect of reasoning. Alchemy, for example, resorts to such poetic wisdom in order to imagine a *lapis philosophorum* that can produce a *coniuntia oppositorum,* harmonizing the disputes among all such elements. Truth becomes a ritual of scenes in which all things can change their images into each other. The transitive category for lead becoming gold transmutes into a redemptive allegory about body becoming soul. The *lapis philosophorum* is a thing unlike any other, but it makes things so that they are like everything else. It is the metaphor for all metaphor.

Donne practices the poetic wisdom of such a scenic ritual when he deliberately misunderstands the difference between the science of alchemy and his poetry of conceits, inviting his reader, "As fire these drossie Rymes to purifie, / Or as Elixir, to change them to gold" since such a reader is "that Alchimist which alwaies had / Wit, whose one spark could make good things of bad" ([1633] 1985, 294). Alchemy becomes a metaphor that can undergo a process of alchemy itself. The device of the conceit reflects an alchemical marriage of antonymical extremes so that, for example, the idea of love can be equated with any motif, no matter how absurd, be it a drafting compass or a drinking insect. The lapis of alchemy, like the lexis of poetry, reveals that the figural is merely the alembic for the literal. The noble metal of truth arises from the ignoble filth of error.[5]

Vico claims that, just as modern science shows that "man becomes all things by understanding (*homo intelligendo fit omnia*)," so also does poetic wisdom show that "man becomes all things by *not* understanding . . . (*homo non intelligendo fit omnia*)" ([1744] 1984, 130). To understand on behalf of truth is to be reactive, accepting the world of the *as is,* but to misunderstand on behalf of error is to be creative, inventing the world of the *as if.* To be an alchemist is to practice an aesthetic that acts as a *lapis philosophorum,* transmuting the errors of alchemy (a nomad science) into the truths of chemistry (a royal science), but ironically, this change requires that science and poetry shift from an order where they are unified to an order where they are divided. A literal stone that philosophers must diligently seek embodies a figural power that they must eventually deny.

Foucault argues that, during such a transition, the "tautological world of resemblance now finds itself dissociated and, as it were, split down the middle" ([1969] 1973, 58). For Donne, such a dissociation of sensibility implies the failure of alchemy to reconcile the imminent conflict between the subjective affect of imagining and the objective effect of reasoning: "new philosophy cals all in doubt" so that "[t]he Sun is lost, and th'earth, and no man's wit / Can well direct him, where to looke for it" ([1611] 1985, 335). The old, geocentric order of elemental synthesis regards the conceit as the integral epitome of all similes, but the new, heliocentric order of empirical analysis regards the conceit as the marginal extreme of all follies.[6] Not until the advent of 'pataphysics does the conceit, the synthesis of opposites, regain its status as a device of poetic wisdom.

The Mechanismic Phase

Bacon observes that, before empiricism, "systems are but so many stage plays, representing worlds of their own creation after an unreal and scenic fashion" ([1620] 1960, 49). Natural history must revoke these "Idols of the Theater" (49), replacing the theatrical world of scenes (the *as if*) with the empirical world of senses (the *as is*), but this change risks an aporia since this new mode of investigation only ratifies a new mode of dramatization — the *petit récit* of an experiment, in which an event must restage itself again and again under the auspice of control. Epistemic errors are now simply traced to linguistic abuses. Science in its mechanismic phase sees that signs exist only by being known: they are written onto things by culture, and they distinguish the distance between things in order to invent the synchronic continuum of their proper order.

Reality for the mechanismic phase is a stable clock that operates within a static regimen. Knowing such a reality involves a mathetic function, testing signs, disquisiting them, regimenting them within a diagram that displays all their modes of identity and alterity. Such a taxonomy of forms distributes signs incrementally throughout a royal regime in which all things must depend upon an order of both equivalence and difference. The evidence of science, not the eminence of poetry, provides a consensus for the verities of a paradigm. All texts have their truthfulness at stake. All texts must legitimate their sources. The truth of science fulfills such a requisite by favorably gauging its power over the object against the divine power of nature. The truth of science thus aligns its cause, its *arche,* with the power of a noumenal origin.

Modern science simply colonizes the alterity of the object, leaving no space for poetic wisdom to speak the truth about nature except through an act of alliance with such a norm. Poetic wisdom must adopt the values of modern science in order to state any objective verities. Sprat, for example, argues that, poetically, "*Truth* is never so well express'd or amplify'd, as by those Ornaments which are *Tru[e]* and *Real* in themselves" ([1667] 1958, 414). Truth is the best ornament because it has the least ornament—which is to say that science is the best poetry because it has the least poetry. The irony here is that verse must learn its rules of metaphor from a genre that rules out metaphor. The sage of science actually becomes the muse of poetry (hence the numerous elegies to scientists, particularly Newton, despite the fact that science follows a principle of antipoeisis).[7]

Newton berates poetry for its "ingenius nonsense" (Bush 1950, 40) even though Glover portrays him as the paragon of poetry: "O might'st thou, ORPHEUS, now again revive, / And NEWTON should inform thy list'ning ear" ([1728] 1972, [23]). Poetry indulges in scientific sycophancy, largely because the gravity of force in the *Principia* lends itself to the idea of a poetic sublime just as the levity of light in the *Opticks* lends itself to the idea of a poetic beauty.[8] Glover writes that "Newton demands the muse" ([1728] 1972, [14]), but soon Thomson wonders: "How shall the Muse, then, grasp the mighty theme," particularly "when but a few / Of the deep-studying race can stretch their minds / To what he knew" (1853, 337). Science has unveiled so many universal mysteries that, ironically, it threatens to become a poetry of truth more sublime than the truth of poetry itself.

Poetry makes an effort to dispute this omniscience of science (its will to power), as Swift does, for example, but poetry cannot dispute the conscience of science (its will to truth). While science ascends to a state of greater complexity, becoming more abstract, theoretic, and autocratic, poetry descends through science to a state of greater simplicity, becoming more concrete, pragmatic, and democratic. To keep pace with science, poetry must shift its focus from the sublime in the natural physics of Newton to the beauty in the natural history of Linnaeus. As Aikin avers, the updated images of natural history must replace the outdated tropes of poetry since "nothing can be really beautiful which has not truth for its basis" ([1777] 1970, 25). To fulfill a didactic mandate, poetry must learn its truth directly from the mineral, the vegetal, and the bestial.[9]

Darwin, the poetic savant, follows such advice to the letter when he explains the botanical taxonomy of Linnaeus by equating modes of floral procreation with modes of social flirtation: "the general design . . . is to inlist Imagination under the banner of Science; and to lead her votaries from the looser analogies, which dress . . . poetry, to the stricter ones, which form . . . philosophy" (1791, v). Poetic pleasure submits to noetic pedagogy. The catalog of flowers—the anthology, so to speak—is merely the flowery ornament for the summary document of its scientific marginalia. The poetry acts as a mere note for the notes themselves—a pretense to plant the seeds of interest so that the reader might in turn disseminate this information. The poetry literally is a botanic garden, in which germinates the romantic metaphor that poetry is organic.

The Organismic Phase

Coleridge observes that, after empiricism, the botanic model of science does inform a poetry of organic unity, but contrary to Darwin, this poetic pleasure does not submit to noetic pedagogy: "[a] poem . . . is opposed to . . . science, by proposing for its *immediate* object pleasure, not truth" ([1817] 1913, 164). Wordsworth qualifies this statement by arguing that "the knowledge of both the Poet and the Man of science is pleasure" ([1802] 1965, 456), but while poetry is an ecstatic search for an intimate truth, science is a monastic search for an ultimate truth—one whose discourse values an empiricism of the senses at the expense of their sensualism. Science in its organismic phase sees that signs evolve by being known: they are written across events by culture, and they distinguish the interval between events in order to direct the diachronic continuum of their normal order.

Reality for the organismic phase is a simple engine that generates a stable dynamic. Knowing such a reality involves an anamnestic function, working signs, implementing them, redeploying them within a program that displays all their modes of function and relation. Such an economy of forms distributes its signs pragmatically throughout a royal regime in which all things must depend upon an order of both productivity and applicability. Not only the evidence of science, but also the progress of science, provides a consensus for the verities of a paradigm. All texts have their usefulness at stake. All texts must legitimate their intents. The truth of science fulfills such a requisite by favorably gauging its power over the subject against the humane power of culture. The truth of science thus aligns its effect, its *telos,* with the power of a noumenal motive.

Modern science simply colonizes the identity of the subject, leaving no space for poetic wisdom to speak the truth about culture except through an act of defiance against such a norm. Poetic wisdom must evict the values of modern science in order to state any subjective verities. Hence, Keats condemns Newton for the "cold philosophy" that must "Conquer all mysteries by rule and line" ([1820] 1959, 226) just as Blake condemns Newton for the "Reasonings like vast Serpents" that must hang their "iron scourges over Albion" ([1804] 1952, 16). Such reasoning that allegedly discredits imagining only creates an undead truth, an ur-Frankenstein that, for Wordsworth, must await a poetic rebirth: "the Poet will lend his divine spirit to aid in the transfiguration" when "science, thus familiarized to men, shall be ready to put on, as it were, a form of flesh and blood" ([1802] 1965, 456).[10]

Wordsworth claims that "[t]he remotest discoveries of the Chemist, the Botanist, or Mineralogist, will be as proper objects of the Poet's art . . . if the time should ever come when these things shall be familiar to us" ([1802] 1965, 456), but in the meantime, this differend has no terms for consensus. Poetry indulges in scientific controversy, largely because the schism between reasoning and imagining has begun to reflect the anomie of poetic labor. For T. H. Huxley, such labor cannot compete with the capital values of utility (1948, 49)—thus poetry must warrant a Benthamite rejection—but for Arnold, such labor does reflect upon the communal values of liberty (1889, 112)—which is to say that the reasoning of science can teach what is real and true, but only the imagining of poetry can teach what is fine and just.

Schlegel writes that poetry must redeem science in the belief that "all art should become science and all science art" ([1797] 1971, 157). Poetry must become a genre of therapeutic knowledge, creating "pseudostatements" that can, according to Richards, detach the untruth of poetry from belief and yet retain the beauty of such untruth in order to refine belief itself (1926, 61). Newtonian cosmology has discredited the poetic object just as Darwinian evolution has discredited the poetic subject; therefore, poetry must henceforth resort to the *as if* of an imaginary solution in order to speak its own truth. Poetry must ascend through science to a state of greater complexity, becoming more abstract, theoretic, and autocratic. Poetry must transform its scientific radicalism, shifting its critique from an opposition (external to science) to a subversion (internal to science).

'Pataphysics thus arises just before modernism begins to wring its hands about the enigma of what Snow calls "the Two Cultures" (1959, 2). Aldous Huxley argues that, despite their dispute, the two cultures resemble each other most when the noetic clarity of reasoning and the poetic opacity of imagining approach the sublimity of the ineffable (1963, 14). What is sublime in the pseudo of poetry can, according to Richards, return reasoning and imagining to an equilibrium that resembles the tension of forces in a cloud of magnets (1926, 15–18).[11] Such an equation of antonyms revives the conceit as a sublime device not of alchemical marriage, but of scientific synthesis; hence, Eliot can equate poetry with a platinum catalyst that fuses oxygen and sulphur without changing itself: "[i]t is in this depersonalization that art may be said to approach the condition of science" (1950, 7).[12]

The Cyborganismic Phase

Barthes observes that, after modernism, science can no longer stabilize its object within an allotelic economy of monosemic reference but must, like poetry, criticize its method within an autotelic economy of polysemic existence: "science speaks itself; literature writes itself . . . : it is not the same body, and hence the same desire, which is behind the one and the other" ([1984] 1986, 5); nevertheless, "science will become literature, insofar as literature . . . is already . . . science" (10), only when science can see that its own truth exists not outside of language, but only because of language. Science in its cyborganismic phase sees that signs evolve beyond being known: they are written as events by culture, and they extinguish the interval between events in order to create the synchronic discontinuum of their random order.

Reality for the cyborganismic phase is a complex matrix that computes a mobile dynamic. Knowing such a reality involves a catamnestic function, playing signs, deregulating them, recombining them within a hologram that displays all their modes of seduction and simulation. Such a synonymy of forms distributes its signs excrementally throughout a nomad regime in which all things must depend upon an order of virtuosity and virtuality. All texts have their artfulness at stake. All texts must legitimate not only their reasons (be they in the origin or in the result) but also the reason for these reasons. The truth of science can no longer fulfill such a requisite by favorably gauging its power against the metaphysics of either an *arche* or a *telos*, but only against the 'pataphysics of an exceptional phenomenon—be it an *excess*, a *chiasm*, or a *swerve*.

Modern science simply monopolizes the totality of both the subject and the object, leaving no space for poetic wisdom to speak the truth for itself except as an act of deviance within such a norm. Modern science can no longer stabilize the disparity between the subjective affect of imagining and the objective effect of reasoning. The advent of 'pataphysics signals the first attempts to subvert this agenda from within its own limits. The science of 'pataphysics inspires a literary tradition that has in turn begun to regard itself as a response to science with an outcome to be studied by a science, be it formalist, structural, semiologic, or cybernetic.[13] The 'pataphysical fundamentals of surrationalism have in turn provided the aesthetic parallel for the dialectic sophistry of almost all antimetaphysical metaphilosophies.

Baudrillard suggests that, "a century after Jarry, but in a cool universe without irony, and without 'pataphysical acid," science has so inflated the fund of information that the excesses of such metastasis evoke the *gidouille* of Ubu: "['p]ataphysics or metaphysics, this pregnancy . . . is one of the strangest signs . . . of this spectral environment where each cell (each function, each structure), is left with the possibility, as in cancer, . . . of multiplying indefinitely" ([1983] 1990a, 28). Science is a tautological extravagance for which Ubu, "a figure of genius, replete with that which has absorbed everything, transgressed everything, . . . radiates in the void like an imaginary solution" (71). Science now functions in what Jarry might call an economy of *phynance* ([1944] 1969, 43), expending without investing, producing *pschitt* or *merdre*—an ironic eponym for "excess" with an excess letter.

Baudrillard suggests, that for such an economy of science, the threat of the unreal haunts every system of verity since the methods of physics can no longer confirm whether or not reality itself is a fantasy: "[s]uch would be the [']pataphysics . . . that lies in wait for all physics at its inadmissible limits" ([1983] 1990a, 85). Has not physics already started to resemble a science of imaginary solutions, what with its particle zoo of new paradoxes (the amphibolies of particles, the metaleptics of causality)? Do we not see a hint of 'pataphysics in the strangeness of antimatter, black holes, and time travel (the theories of which have already fomented philosophical apprehensions about the existence of existence itself)? In the face of such scientific absurdities, poetry has responded by portraying itself as a literalized experiment.

Prigogine and Stengers observe that, for such an episteme, "science occupies a peculiar position, that of a poetical interrogation of nature, in the etymological sense that the poet is a 'maker'—active," inventing the world ex post facto while observing the world a priori (1984, 301). Science has finally achieved the hyperbole of its own "death," so to speak, disappearing into a condition of tautological metalepsis, paradoxically becoming both the cause and the effect of its own virtual reality. Science has begun to fulfill the simulacral precession that, for Baudrillard, defines the 'pataphysics of a postmodern philosophy.[14] As Genosko suggests, [i]t is surely a [']pataphysical accident that death is for Baudrillard the very . . . gesture which pushes the tautologies of the system over the edge, with a belly laugh of symbolic proportions" (1994, 116).

Pseudo Sciences

Feyerabend argues that, for science to progress, the nomic truth of the *as is* must induce an escape to the ludic space of an *as if:* "*we need a dreamworld in order to discover the features of the real world . . . which may actually be just another dream-world*" (1978, 32). Science in such a *Traumwelt* adopts not the terrorism of unified theories but the anarchism of ramified theories—"[t]he only principle that does not inhibit progress is: *anything goes*" (23). Such a principle does not encode a laissez-faire economy (whose Darwinian competition requires that a royal science discard the truth of a defunct concept as either extinct or deviant); instead, such a principle tries to entice a savoir-faire economy (whose Lucretian arbitration requires that a nomad science bracket the truth of a defunct concept as either dormant or defiant).[15]

'Pataphysics dramatizes this principle of Feyerabend by arguing that, however obsolete or indiscrete any theory might at first appear, every theory has the potential to improve knowledge in some way. Just as biodiversity can make an ecology more adaptable, so also can dilettantism make an episteme more versatile. The process of science must learn to place its defunct concepts into a kind of suspended animation that preserves them for the millenary reverie of an imaginary science. The truth diverges throughout many truths, inducing the sophisms of dissent, novelty, and paradox: "given any rule . . . for science, there are always circumstances when it is advisable not only to ignore the rule, but to adopt its opposite" (Feyerabend 1978, 23) in order "*to make the weaker case the stronger . . . and thereby to sustain the motion of the whole*" (30).

'Pataphysics thus behaves as if it is a *Philosophie des Als Ob*. Vaihinger observes that the phrase "as if" constitutes a "comparative apperception" ([1911] 1966, 91), juxtaposing two concepts somewhere in the interzone between the virtuality of a figural relation and the actuality of a literal equation. Neither rhetorical nor theoretical, the *as if* constitutes a paradox of contingency, since reference is made to an impossibility, but from this impossibility an inference is made: "reality . . . is *compared* with something whose . . . unreality is at the same time admitted" (98). The *as if* posits the possible consequences of an impossible inconsequence. The *as if* is simply the imaginary solution to the question *what if*. Is not this question a deliberate misreading that shows the real and the true to be quasi and pseudo—free, that is, to be something else?

Metaphysics forgets that the operative conditional (*as if*) is not an imperative conditional (*if then*); nevertheless, the latter relation always resides unheard in the former relation. The *if then* revokes the suspension of disbelief in the *as if* so that an event must be treated as it would be treated if it were *as is*. The slightness of this difference between the *as if* and the *if then* marks the slightness of the difference between truth and power. The 'pataphysician explores such conditionals, wondering what might happen when we pretend that science is poetry or that poetry is science (*as if* these two terms are philosophically interchangeable). The 'pataphysician dreams that, like the *ur* from Tlön, such exceptional occurrences in philosophy might become less fantastic, more realistic—until they seem more real than real, making reality itself nothing more than a figment of our imagination.

2. Millennial 'Pataphysics
The Poetics of an Imaginary Science

The Millenary Problem

'Pataphysics has so far proven daunting to critics because of its academic frivolity and hermetic perversity; consequently, critics have often defined 'pataphysics as more problematic than theorematic, reading Jarry only by focusing on the dramaturgy of his life, not on the philosophy of his work— as if *how he lived* is more artful than *what he wrote*. Few critics have recognized that, far from simply being the idiolect of an alcoholic, 'pataphysics is a surrational perspective that has had an extensive, yet forgotten, influence upon the canonic history of radical poetics. Few critics have recognized that 'pataphysics actually informs the innovation of the postmodern. Not only does this avant-garde pseudoscience valorize whatever is exceptional and paralogical; it also sets the parameters for the contemporary relationship between science and poetry.

Jarry may precede the French word *'pataphysique* with an apostrophe in order to avoid punning, but ironically, his neologism is still polysemic, since the French idiom for the English word "flair," *la patte* (the hand, or "paw," of the artist) appears in the homophonic phrase *patte à physique*—the flair of physics: Ubu, for example, is a slapstick comedian (*pataud physique*) of unhealthy obesity (*pâteux physique*), whose bodily language (*patois physique*) foments an astounded physics (*épatée physique*) that is not your physics (*pas ta physique*). The apostrophe denotes that, while wordplay in the sciences

27

is absent by edict, it is still present by proxy, since even the search for truth is a language-game that can never efface its status as a language-game. As Torma avers, "[t]he word *true* means precisely nothing here and succumbs under a [']pataphysical paw-swipe" ([1929] 1995, 145).

Jarry argues that, for 'pataphysics, reality does not exist except as a comparative apperception, in which a 'pataphysician might conjure a reality to explore—almost as if "[t]he world was simply an immense ship" ([1897] 1989, 103)—a sieve, perhaps, with a 'pataphysician at the helm. Baudrillard argues that, for "Jarryites," all such denials of reality (including those now cited in quantum physics) entail a fantasy about the omnipotence of thought—its power to dream events into being, to change the world through the *ur* of simulation ([1983] 1990a, 80). As McCaffery suggests when explicating 'pataphysics: "[b]eyond mendacity . . . is the vitality of articulation which carries its own positive implications: that all events are capable of alteration, that a lie attacks language at its weakest fabricative point: reality itself" (1986, 200).

'Pataphysics uses such sophistic reasoning in order to suggest that the ability of science to repeat its results, to foment new advances, is fortuitous, since it is gratuitous, given that no necessity determines whether or not reality has to be representable or even comprehensible to any viewpoint. Sandomir, for example, adopts this stance when he suggests that, because "Existence has no more reason to exist than reason has to exist" and because "the manifestations of existence are aberrant and their necessity entirely contingent," a 'pataphysician might easily argue that " 'Pataphysics precedes Existence" (1960d, 170) insofar as such a science creates in advance the reality that it explores. For Jarry, science is nothing more than a tautological recursiveness that only finds what it seeks: a reality that proves itself to be both existent and rational.

A Scientific Classicism

Initially lampooning the curriculum of the physics master Père Hébert at the Lycée de Rennes, 'pataphysics subsequently evolves in a fragmentary manner through three political contexts of literary personae: Ubu (who mocks the power of a monarch); Sengle (who mocks the power of a soldier); and Faustroll (who mocks the power of a scholar)—all three attacking the quiddity of both the real and the true in order to show that, when faced with relativistic perspectives, "[u]niversal assent is [an] incomprehensible prejudice" (Jarry [1911] 1965, 192). Jarry develops this precept most expansively in his "Neo-Scientific Novel" about Faustroll, whose absurd voyage aboard a sieve takes him to the realm of Ethernity, where his exploits lampoon some of the popular science of the fin de siècle, particularly the hydrodynamic lectures of Boys and the thermodynamic lectures of Kelvin.

Jarry parodies the discourse of such scientific luminaries, who attempt to demonstrate the utility of science through the dramaturgic performance of a mechanical experiment. Rather than build operative devices for harnessing thought (as Boys and Kelvin might do), the 'pataphysician must instead build excessive devices for unleashing thought—devices like the urinary jet, which trills music, or the robotic sun, which churns flame: the former machine distorting the work of Boys, who must explain the sonic resonation of fluid propulsion by referring to a mechanism built from glass tubes, rubber sheets, and water jets (Boys [1902] 1959, 103); the latter machine distorting the work of Kelvin, who must explain the mechanical tropes of solar convection by referring to a mechanism built from paddle wheels, screw gears, and pulley winches (Kelvin 1889, 379).

Jarry imagines such parodic devices in order to sabotage the Newtonian classicism that has traditionally characterized the epistemological differentiation between physics and metaphysics. Rather than subject the emergent sciences of both hydrodynamics and thermodynamics to the problematic determinism of a mechanical philosophy (as Boys and Kelvin might do), Jarry attempts instead to accentuate the surrational potentials of such physics so that what is random and absurd might fulfill the anomalous imperative of a cyborganic philosophy. While Kelvin describes reality as a liquid system of springs and weights, whose gyrostatic elasticity approaches an inexorable condition of inertia (1889, 239), Jarry believes that the avantgarde pseudoscience of 'pataphysics can intervene in the process of such a reality in order to perturb the entropy of its banal order.

Jarry endeavors to demonstrate that, like alchemy, which reduces all *scientia* to an erotic system of symbolic exchange, even the chemical sciences comprise a set of metaphorical abstractions, each laden with its own libidinal intensity. Jarry does not borrow scientific *concepts* so much as scientific *conceits,* doing so, in order to imagine a "counterdynamic," a geometric *catachemy* ([1911] 1965, 253), whose magical symbols can allegedly reconcile the opposition between the axiological objectivity of the ontic world and the mythological subjectivity of the semic world: "the Geometer . . . knowest all things by the means of lines drawn in different directions, and hast given us the veritable portrait . . . of God in three escutcheons which are the quart essence of Tarot symbols" (251). Jarry suggests that, even in science, the figural is merely the alembic of the literal.

A Scientific Radicalism

Jarry may intend to transform the present context of a posited reality, inspiring the anarchic politics of permanent rebellion among much of the avant-garde; nevertheless, such critics as Shattuck and Sandomir have argued at length and with fervor that, because 'pataphysics is an alleged science of indifference, such a science can never support any political intention—unless it supports all of them. Shattuck argues that, because " '[p]ataphysics preaches no rebellion . . . , no political reform," such a science never attempts to change events: "the [']pataphysician . . . suspends all values" (1984, 104). Sandomir likewise argues that, because " '[p]ataphysics does not enlighten any more than it should enlighten," such a science never attempts to improve things: "[b]ecause of this, orgies of salvation are avoided" (1960a, 173).

Shattuck argues that " '[p]ataphysics attempts no cures" (1984, 104) even though Jarry has expanded upon a childhood burlesque of pedagogic authority in order to foment a spirit of revolt, be it antibourgeois or antiphilistine. Although Shattuck may define such a nomad science as a ludic philosophy for stoic epicureans since "[i]t allows each person to live his life as an exception, proving no law but his own" (1984, 106), Shattuck also disarms the radical anarchy of such Nietzschean sentiments in order to equate 'pataphysics with a postmodern will, not of wholehearted iconoclasm but of halfhearted compliance: "the etiquette of 'pataphysics: *ironic conformity*" (1984, 105). Shattuck, however, cannot acknowledge that what he regards as an egalitarian celebration of indifference may instead be nothing more than a parody of our own scientific impartiality.

Sandomir likewise argues that 'pataphysics is apolitical in its incertitude: "although democracy or demophily are . . . only one fiction among others, the [']pataphysician is without doubt the undisputed holder of the absolute record of democracy: without even making an effort he beats the egalitarians at their own game," for "[t]he fact is that he denies nothing; he exsuperates"—"[h]e is not there to do away with things but to subsume them" (1960c, 179). Sandomir, however, does not seem to recognize that, since 'pataphysics studies exceptions in order to make the weaker case the stronger, such irony always engages in a fervent dispute with the power of its present reality—even if such dispute engages what Baudrillard might call the "transpolitical," therein deploying the fatalistic strategies of simulation ([1983] 1990a, 25).

Shattuck and Sandomir may forget that, like Nietzsche, Jarry attempts to radicalize philosophy, not simply to preserve metaphysics through an impotent negation of it but to displace metaphysics through a radical mutation within it. Since Jarry develops 'pataphysics most expansively through Faustroll and his exploits in Ethernity, this survey concentrates upon the third phase of 'pataphysics in order to draw such parallels between Jarry and Nietzsche. The survey then goes on to discuss the three declensions of the exceptional (the *anomalos,* the *syzygia,* and the *clinamen*) in order to itemize their 'pataphysical similarities to modern tropes that have provided a basis for antimetaphysical metaphilosophies—the assumption being that 'pataphysics represents an unwritten but intrinsic intertext to many of the radical tactics found in deconstructive methodologies.

The Modernity of Jarry

'Pataphysics for Jarry resembles the philosophy of Nietzsche, insofar as both writers make a case for *perspectivism.* M. Bourdon at the Lycée de Rennes is known to have taught Jarry the philosophy of Nietzsche before its translation into French (Beaumont 1984, 21), and only a few critics, particularly Dufresne (1993, 26) and McCaffery (1997, 11), have intimated that Nietzsche provides a critically neglected but integrally important set of antecedents for 'pataphysics. Just as Nietzsche has striven *"to look at science in the perspective of the artist"* (1966, 19), greeting all philosophy with skepticism, so also does Jarry combine the noetic and the poetic into a genre that questions all epistemological prerequisites. For Jarry and Nietzsche, knowledge itself is so deceptive that it cannot even be corrected by this knowledge about knowledge.

Perspectivism suggests that reality does not exist, except as the interpretive projection of a phenomenal perspective—which is to say that, for Nietzsche, reality is only the effect of a *Traumwelt,* in which "there are many kinds of 'truths,' and consequently there is no truth" ([1906] 1968, 540) since "[t]ruths are illusions which we have forgotten are illusions" ([1873] 1979, 84). Jarry likewise argues that reality is but one aspect of an Ethernity, in which "there are only hallucinations, or perceptions," and every "perception is an hallucination which is true" ([1897] 1989, 103). Reality is nothing more than a comparative apperception, an *as if* for a disparate collection of different viewpoints, each one creating the true for itself, while opposing every other view. Each perspective is thus a solipsistic singularity that has no recourse to perceptual consensus.[1]

Science, for Nietzsche, is merely a viewpoint that does not explicate a common reality so much as interpret a unique fantasy: "[t]he habits of our senses have woven us into lies and deception of sensation: these are the basis of all our judgments and 'knowledge'," for which "there is absolutely no escape . . . into the real world" (Babich 1994, 89). Science, for Jarry, is also such "a statement of what is visible to the mortal eye (it is always a matter of mortal eyes, hence vulgar and . . . flawed . . . , and the sensory organ being a cause of error, the scientific instrument simply magnifies that sense in the direction of its error)" ([1897] 1989, 105). As Daumal avers, no science can exceed the nooscopic limit of its own anthropic focus, and thus "['p]ataphysics will measure . . . the extent to which everyone is stuck in the rut of individual existence" ([1970] 1995, 33).

Jarry adopts such a solipsistic viewpoint, in which perception "*symbolically attributes the properties of objects, described by their virtuality, to their lineaments*" ([1911] 1965, 193), the 'pataphysician willfully mistaking the superficies of the image for the substance of the thing: "he no longer made any distinction at all between his thoughts and actions nor between his dreaming and . . . waking" ([1897] 1989, 103). Just as Nietzsche describes reality as a vacuous surface, in which we grasp "nothing but the mirror" ([1881] 1982, 141), so also does Jarry describe a reality of "parallel mirrors" that reflect their own "reciprocal emptiness" ([1911] 1965, 211). Like Berkeley, both Jarry and Nietzsche argue that *esse* is *percipi,* but while Berkeley posits a panoptic absolute, whose gaze sustains all other views, Jarry and Nietzsche argue that no view is absolute.

'Pataphysics in fact sees that every viewpoint is dissolute—including its own—since no view can offer a norm for all others. Jarry even suggests that, because invisible worlds transect our perceived reality at many points across many scales, the cosmos almost resembles a heteroclite archipelago of monolithic lighthouses—strange islands with their own "obelischolychnies" ([1911] 1965, 201), each of which illuminates a particular haven for its own idiocratic truth.[2] Only eyes adapted to a specific spectrum can detect a given signal; hence, some lights go unseen, particularly by the *hemeralopes,* the dayblind who see only in darkness: "for moles . . . , a lighthouse is as invisible as . . . the infrared rays" (201). A beacon may even sound its alarms at a frequency too extreme for auditory response: "[n]o waves break against it, and thus no sound guides one to it" (201).

'Pataphysics avers that even science itself is just another beacon, one that guides instinct away from a cool, but natural, truth toward a warm, but cultural, truth. Science thus behaves like a wolf that no longer bays at the fire of a terrible moon but only at the glow of an electric lamp. Such a *pharos* may emit light at a different wavelength but does so at an equivalent luminosity, replacing the vulgar idolatry of belief with the more subtle egomania of reason: "[s]cience, say the bourgeois, has dethroned superstition" (Jarry [1897] 1989, 105) when in fact science has simply ensconced itself as the successor to such credulity in order to preside over (*superstare*) the same anthropic biases of these antiquary errors. For every solar truth of a royal science, there is this lunar truth of a nomad science—a forbidden knowledge that history must outshine.

'Pataphysics confronts such a millenary conundrum with imaginary solutions, whose metaphors of exception have perhaps lent as much to Derrida as they have owed to Nietzsche, providing an unwritten intertext for postmodern philosophy. Just as McCaffery has discussed Nietzsche in terms of a "Zarathustran 'Pataphysics" (1997, 11), so also has Dufresne discussed Derrida in terms of a "[D]econstructive [']pataphysics" (1993, 26), and Stillman goes so far as to argue that "Jarry's desire to escape metaphysics returns today, newly masked under the philosophical thrust of deconstruction" (1983, 39) since Jarry offers a poetic theory of contradictory undecidability, continually inverting a dyadic hierarchy, while momentarily subverting its mutual exclusion—neither canceling nor surpassing the dialectic: not *Aufhebung*, but *Steigerung*.

Dufresne observes that "the sheer coincidence . . . which conjoins deconstruction to [']pataphysics is worth further examination" (1993, 29) since "it is here . . . that Derrida, Jarry, and Nietzsche form an unholy trinity, a truly grand . . . style of epiphenomenal proportions" (31)—a style that does not simply claim, as true, that no claim is true, but that tries instead to imagine a *double science,* whose episteme no longer presumes in advance that we even know how to know. As Nietzsche avers, "[o]ne would have to *know* what being is, in order to *decide* whether this or that is real . . . ; in the same way, what *certainty* is, what *knowledge* is, and the like.—But since we do *not* know this, a critique of the faculty of knowledge is senseless: how should a tool be able to criticize itself when it can use only *itself* for critique?" (Babich 1994, 88).

Nietzsche reveals that, for this reason, "the problem of science cannot be recognized on the ground of science" ([1872] 1966, 18) since to do so requires that science be used to prove that it cannot be used to prove. Nietzsche thus evokes the classic paradox that has come to define deconstructive ratiocination. Sandomir has even gone on to affirm that, of all the sciences, "[o]nly 'pataphysics ... does not explain itself but establishes its own position within a vicious circle" (1960b, 176), doing so in order to claim what science cannot admit: that the absurdity of tautology is a condition of knowledge. As Daumal avers, "['p]ataphysical arguments do not necessarily set up systems designed to demonstrate the truth of this or that proposition;" instead, "[t]hey generally develop as *vicious circles* and bring the human spirit to a limit-state of stupor and scandal" ([1970] 1995, 112).

Derrida, for example, does not simply oppose a thesis with its antithesis, nor does he even equate them to a third term of synthesis—nor does Derrida simply invert this system of value between thesis and antithesis but affirms (and denies) both sides of this dialectic, revealing the undecidable contradiction that always appears to make such a relation both possible and impossible at the same time: "[t]he break with this structure of belonging can be announced only through ... a certain *strategic* arrangement which, within the field of metaphysical opposition, uses the strengths of the field to turn its own stratagems against it, producing a force of dislocation that spreads itself throughout the entire system, fissuring it in every direction and thoroughly *delimiting* it" ([1967] 1978, 20).

Jarry, Nietzsche, and Derrida do not defend the truth of their own sophism so much as flout the truisms of truth itself—its self-evidence, its self-awareness. Daumal even observes that "*whatever is self-evident cloaks itself in absurdity as its only means of perceptibility*" — "[w]hence the humorous appearance of [']pataphysical reasoning" ([1970] 1995, 31), whose ludicrous syllogisms lead to an infinitude of simulation: "[']pataphysical sophism is an apparent sophism which envelops an apparent truth which envelops an apparent sophism which envelops an apparent truth, and so on ad infinitum" (111)—or as Torma observes: "*[p]ut metaphysics behind [']pataphysics and you make it merely the facade for a belief*" when in fact "*the essence of [']pataphysics is that it is the facade of a facade, behind which there is nothing*" —only the black abyss of total doubt ([1929] 1995, 145).

The Ethernity of Faustroll

Jarry situates his own 'pataphysical sensibility in such a posited reality, an imaginary dimension that he calls "Ethernity," a "NOWHERE, OR SOMEWHERE, which is the same thing" ([1911] 1965, 248)—an interzone where the reference of a sign does not describe, but conjures, the existence of the real through the *ur* of simulation. Ethernity resembles a state of maximum entropy—a nullified condition whose potential goes unmeasured, unobserved, its eigenstate corresponding to "the perplexity of a man outside time and space, who has lost his . . . measuring rod, and his tuning fork" (248). Like the Maxwell Demon, the 'pataphysician intervenes in such a void of thermodynamic equilibrium, sorting its randomly distributed atoms into narrowly constructed forms (249)—creating, in this case, a spectroscope whose measurements cause a fiat lux ex nihilo.

Ethernity expresses a reality built out of thought alone—a realm whose fantastic substance, "ether," refers not only to the hypothetical medium that can transport light in a vacuum (as is the case for the photic theory of Kelvin) but also to the anesthetic vapor that can transform sight in an addict (as is the case for the mystic vision of Jarry). Whether scientific or mythopoeic, both kinds of ether provide an imaginary solution to the problem of *illumination*. Even light itself must express the ontological expediency of an imagined paradigm. Just as quantum physics has shown that measuring a perception converts a potential into an existence by collapsing a wave function, *realizing* reality rather than reporting it, so also does 'pataphysics reveal that "the function of navigators was to make land" (Jarry [1911] 1965, 199)—not to find it.

Ethernity is simply the milieu for all such imaginary perception, be it a scientific model or a novel literature. Books there become an archipelago, where voyagers can travel together from text to text, as though from isle to isle (be it the land of Cack, of Ptyx, of Her, etc.). Each port of call is a haven for the allegorical impressions of either an artist or a writer, as if such motifs are "excellent quintessences . . . brought back by inquisitive men from their travels" (Jarry [1911] 1965, 203)—for example: "[f]rom Rabelais, the little bells to which the devils danced during the tempest"; "from Lautréamont, the scarab, beautiful as the trembling of hands in alcoholism" (191). Such images provide a *Wunderkammern* of uncanny specimens for an imaginary scientist, who collects as though without exception, all cases of exception— all the rarities of poetic teratism.

Ethernity presents to us a literary universe to be explored by a science that must learn in turn to explore itself as literary; consequently, the exploits of Faustroll in Ethernity resemble the voyages of Gulliver in Laputa or even the adventures of Alice in Wonderland (insofar as all three fantasies use a nomad journey to lampoon a royal science). Swift and Carroll, however, use such nonsense to expose the aporias of the rational on behalf of *reform,* whereas Jarry uses his nonsense to induce his own visions of the schizoid on behalf of *revolt*. What Swift berates in the science of Boyle and Hooke (eclecticism), Jarry admires in the science of Boys and Kelvin. What Carroll debates on the surface with Humpty Dumpty (amphilogism), Jarry extends to the extreme with Bosse-de-Nage. What Alice and Gulliver fear to become (schizonoiac), Faustroll already is.

Faustroll is a 'pataphysical philosopher who has gone beyond good and evil to invoke the reverie of a schizoid superman — a parodic version of Zarathustra, the kind of exceptional personality that Sengle might describe as one of the "superior intelligences, who are few," but who are often mistaken for the infirm or the insane since "the bourgeois is not learned enough to study the body and the scientist is too learned . . . to study the spirit" (Jarry [1897] 1989, 106). The *Ubermensch* defies all such Manicheanism, fusing the soul of a supernal "Faust" with the body of an infernal "Troll," [3] parodying the telic myths of Darwinian evolution by collating beast, human, and deity into an apostate "tetragon" (Jarry [1911] 1965, 254) — the Mephistophelian image of an hermaphroditic satyr, for whom God is just an artifice of humanity — "man to an improper degree" ([1911] 1965, 183).[4]

Faustroll is quite literally a literary creation, his body becoming a book — a papyrus cadaver that can unscroll to divulge the secrets of a poetic vision, his eyes, like "two capsules of ordinary writing-ink" (Jarry [1911] 1965, 183). Just as Jarry makes a spectacle of himself, adopting the mannerisms of his characters (particularly Ubu), so also does the *Ubermensch* embody 'pataphysics through the syntax of his own corpus — a *gidouille* perhaps, which charts "the progress of the solid future entwined . . . in spirals" so that, "[l]ike a musical score, all art and all science were written in the curves . . . , and their progression to an infinite degree was prophesied therein" (245). For such a superman, whose life is a text that displays the grammar of flux and flow, language itself becomes an absurd vessel — a sieve of words, set adrift upon the oceanic surface of a protean reality.

Faustroll indeed sets sail in such a ship, whose manifest does not itemize the ballast of a boat so much as the content of a book: its hypertext of influence — a literal "network" where the science of Boys and the poetry of Lear can fuse into a conceit about language. While Lear writes nonsense about the Jumblies, who "went to sea in a Sieve, they did, / In a Sieve they went to sea" ([1871] 1947, 71), Boys proves that, despite such an absurd notion, the surface tension of water can indeed support a sieve: "[t]his experiment . . . illustrates how difficult it is to write . . . perfect nonsense" ([1902] 1959, 29). Boys, however, does not make sense of a poem so much as get stuck in its mesh. For Jarry, such a sieve is also a trope for a semiotic gridwork — a chart riven with holes, its network able to rest upon the superficies of reality but unable to hold its substance.

Faustroll regards this reality as the surface tension of either an elastic film or a crystal skin—whatever constitutes a superficial experience, whose solipsism requires a *mathesis singularis* in order to accommodate the specificity of each perspective. Regular science must standardize such experience, according to the substantive metaphysics of a capital economy, so that each viewpoint can be replicated and substituted for every other viewpoint. Units of scale function like rates of value in a monetary standard so that to measure is to judge the whole by one piece—to make one case of exception the basis for all other conceptions. The science of 'pataphysics, however, expresses amazement at the very arbitrariness of such measurement, arguing that the generality of such standards must always efface the speciality of any anomalies.

Faustroll defies this demand for uniform metrics by acting out a spectacle of hyperbolic exactitude, forcing each unique standard to an extreme beyond all standards (hence his absurd use of decimal exponents and quantum diameters as units of scale). He suggests that, if science must pretend that its measure is no caprice, then the act of defining a unit of nondensity according to a quantity of vacuum seems far less arbitrary than the act of defining a unit of density according to a quantity of water (Jarry [1911] 1965, 193). Is not measurement just a morbid drive to abolish the irony of such a vacuum, be it astronomical or infinitesimal—the very irony that is the abyss of 'pataphysics itself? Is not science afraid to admit its own cognitive innumeracy when faced with the abysmal vertigo, if not the *horror vacui,* in the void of such a *Traumwelt?*[5]

'Pataphysics argues that every truth of science depends upon such questions of scale, be they micro or macro (like the schism in physics between atomic laws and cosmic laws). Crookes, for example, has argued that a shift in scale might cause an observer to mistake both capillary action and Brownian motion for forces stronger than gravity (1897, 609). Citing Swift, Crookes even says that the ability to study thermal combustion under secure conditions may depend upon the dimensions of an observer: for Lilliputians, chemistry fails because they can generate only insufficient heat; for Brobdingnagians, chemistry fails because they can generate only superabundant heat (611). Citing Crookes, Jarry in turn uses this imagery to explain 'pataphysical perspectivism, depicting Faustroll as a miniature homunculus who changes size in order to explore the surface of a leaf.

Surface tension, when experienced at a such a small scale, causes water to become a plastic solid rather than an aqueous fluid, a "malleable glass" (Jarry [1911] 1965, 195), whose exploded droplets are not wet and soft but dry and hard, like diamonds. The miniaturized 'pataphysician reveals that even a raindrop can contain a microcosm, "a globe, twice his size, through whose transparency the outlines of the universe appeared to him gigantically enlarged, whilst his own image, reflected dimly . . . , was magnified" (195). The droplet is a metaphor for the eye itself, a fluid sphere, an "ovoid myopia," whose lens does not inspect the real so much as distort it, each drop "drawing along beneath it the image of the tangential point of the universe . . . , magnifying its fabulous center" (195)—in this case, the alibi for a phantasmal solipsism: the image of man himself.

Nietzsche argues that, when such a science studies the real, science admires the true, not because the true grants itself either a use or an aim, but because the true treats itself as both a law and an end: "the faith in science, which after all exists undeniably, cannot owe its origin to such a calculus of utility; it must have originated in spite of the fact that the . . . dangerousness of 'the will to truth,' of 'truth at any price' is proved to it constantly" ([1882] 1974, 281). The will to truth entails, but effaces, its own will to error. For 'pataphysics, the threat of error finds itself expressed through the three declensions of exception (the *anomalos,* the *syzygia,* and the *clinamen*)— three events that involve a monstrous encounter, be it in the form of an excess, a chiasm, or a swerve—whatever takes on the character of alterity in the aftermath of some accident.

Anomalos: **The Principle of Variance**

Anomalos is the first declension of exception: the anomaly of the *excess.* Differing from every other thing in a system that values the norm of equivalence, it serves the will to disrupt. Jarry may posit this notion within his own modernist context (the *Ausnahme* in Nietzsche or perhaps even the Excluded in Fort), but such a principle of variance does provide a pretext for postmodern philosophy about the theme of paralepsis (e.g., the supplement in Derrida or the parasite in Serres)—excesses that replace what they augment, operating against but within the limits of the system that must exclude them. The *anomalos* is the repressed part of a rule which ensures that the rule does not work. It is a *difference which makes a difference* and is thus synonymous with the cybernetic definition of interferential information— the very measure of surprise.

Nietzsche argues that, wherever life seems repetitive, poetry fulfills a desire for freedom, but wherever life seems disruptive, science fulfills a desire for boredom: "the first instinct of the knower is to *search for rules,* although naturally enough with the confirmation of a rule nothing is as yet 'known'!—[f]rom this we get the superstition of the physicists"—"[t]hey feel 'secure': but behind this intellectual security stands the calming of frightfulness: *they want rules* because these strip the world of its fearsomeness" (Babich 1994, 97).[6] What repeats has a certain order: it is an expected case, a *reprise,* and thus poses no problem, because it implies the security of a paradigm—but what does not repeat has an uncertain order: it is an excepted case, a *surprise,* and thus poses a problem, because it implies the insecurity of a paralogy.

Nietzsche argues that " '[t]hings' do not behave regularly, according to a *rule*" ([1906] 1968, 634). Rules do not curate events so much as defend us from their threat. Rules do not describe the anomaly of our reality so much as restrain the anxiety of its mystery: "[l]et us beware of saying that there are laws in nature" for "[t]here are only necessities" ([1882] 1974, 168)—there is no decree, no thrall, no mutiny. Rules are simply induced as an expedient, not of cognizance but of ignorance. For this reason, Jarry criticizes the truth of such rules by arguing that, while "[m]ost people have seen a certain phenomenon precede or follow some other phenomenon most often, and conclude therefrom that it will ever be thus . . . , this is true only in the majority of cases, depends upon the point of view, and is codified only for convenience—if that" ([1911] 1965, 193).

Jarry argues that the laws of the universe are not laws but "correlations of exceptions, albeit more frequent ones, but in any case accidental data, which reduced to the status of unexceptional exceptions, possess no longer even the virtue of originality" ([1911] 1965, 193). Rules must efface the idiocracy of the *anomalos,* but ironically such a rule about rules already risks the anomaly of paradox itself. While a metaphysical science must rule out exceptions, such exceptions are the rule (in which case they are no longer exceptions); instead, *the rule is itself the exception* in a 'pataphysical science that rules out the rule. The science of 'pataphysics delights in such paradoxes because its logic studies what logic exempts. As Nietzsche avers, "there actually are things to be said in favor of the exception *provided that it never wants to become the rule*" ([1882] 1974, 131).

Fort dramatizes this principle of variance in a kind of 'pataphysical encyclopedia, whose itinerary bombards its Victorian readers with bizarrerie, ironically documenting, as though without exception, cases of exception, be they climatological (tiny frogs, for example, falling from temperate skies) or archaeological (iron tools, for example, hailing from Neolithic times) — case after case, in which science ignores evidence in order to make aberrances fit the procrustean.[7] His parodic theories about the *as if* of extraterrestrial interventionism offer a forum not to decode exceptional phenomena but to debunk scientific prejudice. No theorem, only decorum, prevents science from considering the possibility of such an alien visit. Is not this visit but a trope for the arrival of anomaly itself? Is not truth but a dogma that must *alienate* the *anomalos?*

Anomaly is, after all, like a stranger, estranged. Whether damned (as in Fort), accursed (as in Bataille), or abject (as in Kristeva), such anomaly refers to the anomie of an excess, whose ambiguities transgress the rule that divides identity from alterity.[8] For Baudrillard, however, this metaphysics of anomie may not apply to a 'pataphysics of excess because "[a]nomaly is at play in an aleatory, statistical field . . . of variations and modulations which no longer know . . . transgression" ([1983] 1990a, 26). For metaphysics, the *anomalos* is an infraction of a limit (a difference in specie), but for 'pataphysics, the *anomalos* is an aberration from a curve (a difference in degree). The *anomalos* is a surprise, a mutation — a "simple apparition" without tragedy or perfidy (26). Not criminalized, but relativized, it reveals that everything has the potential to be anomalous.

Faustroll even goes so far as to define reality itself as "*that which is the exception to oneself*" (Jarry [1911] 1965, 245), just as Nietzsche might suggest that, because this universe constitutes an unlikely condition among an infinity of more probable potential, "[t]he astral order in which we live is an exception," whose situation and duration has made possible "an exception of exceptions: the formation of the organic" ([1882] 1974, 168). Such an *anomalos* is the result not of chance design but of random errors — events whose element of surprise brings every rule to life in a reprise without either purpose or refrain. Such an *anomalos* dares science to reconsider its margin of error ($\pm$), the trivial discrepancy between diverse experiments, so that we might in turn imagine a universe where nothing happens twice — instead each event arises from its own set of exclusive accidents.

Syzygia: The Principle of Alliance

Syzygia is the second declension of exception: the syzygy of the *chiasm*. Differing from every other thing in a system that values the norm of difference — it serves the will to confuse. Jarry may posit this notion within a medieval context (the *Coniunctia* of Avicenna or perhaps even the *Myste-*

rium of Paracelsus), but such a principle of alliance does provide a pretext for postmodern philosophy about the theme of syncretism (e.g., the *chiasmus* in Derrida or the *syzygy* in Serres) — conceits which conjoin as much as they disjoin, inverting, while equating, the values of the binary that must support them. The *syzygia* is the neglected part of a pair which ensures that such a pair is neither united nor parted for more than an instant. It coincides with the laughter that erupts when we eliminate differences in order to imagine the incompossible.

Jarry uses the *syzygia* to describe the synthesis of the poetic and the noetic, as derived from a fragment, so that, "during the syzygy of words . . . , one could have reconstructed, through this facet, all art and all science" ([1911] 1965, 245). The word "syzygy" normally refers to a celestial alignment of three planets, two of which are at the opposite antipodes of their orbit around a third. The horizon that connects the two extremes of perihelion and aphelion can provide a conceit for the dualism of conceit itself — the *coniunctia oppositorum* not only between a positive and its negative (*this, notthis*), but also between such a binary relation and its plenary opposite. The syzygy of words reveals that language not only defines but also deletes this distance between extremes. It assumes the possibility of the incompossible: Plus-and-Minus (±).

Jarry suggests that, for "the dispute between the sign Plus and the sign Minus," a philosopher can demonstrate "the identity of opposites by means of the mechanical device called the *physick-stick*" ([1911] 1965, 252). More excremental than instrumental, this symbol of power lampoons phallogocentric representation. Not a priapic scepter, but a toilet brush — such a staff is an "uprooted phallus" ([1894] 1965, 111) that beats the nomad koan, not the royal word, into its student. The device spins about its axis along a line that does not trace out the cross of the law so much as cross out all trace of the law: "in each quarter of every one of your rotations . . . you form a cross with yourself" (111). The device in motion both affirms and negates, becoming not only an alchemical cipher for the holism of opposite parts but also a scientific symbol for a margin of probable error.

Lyotard also refers to this turning of a "bar which separates the this from the not-this" ([1974] 1993, 15), a bar whose stasis signifies a mandatory division but whose motion activates an aleatory confusion.[9] Just as Lyotard implies that such conjugality of revolution can erase the temporality of difference, so also does Jarry argue that the physick-stick is a crankshaft for a time machine, whose syzygy reveals that "there are neither nights nor days," neither systole nor diastole — no "pendulum movements" ([1897] 1989, 103), only this intense instant, atemporal and libidinal. As Jarry argues: minus sign is feminine; plus sign is masculine—"[f]or the Geometer, these two signs cancel each other out or impregnate each other, and there results . . . their progeny, which becomes . . . zero, all the more identical because they are contrary" ([1911] 1965, 252).

Daumal implies that such a *syzygia* repeats an Eastern intuition, insofar as the equation of *this* and *not-this* resembles what Hindus call *Advaita*— the negated duality, in which "To know X = to know (Everything - X)" ([1970] 1995, 31). While "[g]etting this idea into your head will help you get a firm footing in [']Pataphysics" (31), such an idea has often evoked only the mystical vulgarism of the New Age, in which the likes of Capra and Zukav can now popularize the similarity between the Taoist mysticism of the East and the quantum mechanics of the West (so that, for example, the relationship between yin and yang now offers an Asian metaphor for the ambivalences of particle and waveform). For Daumal, the absurdity of such extremes and their equation is laughable—but this laughter is itself what negates dualism and affirms syzygy, like a joyful wisdom.[10]

Daumal writes that " '[p]ataphysical laughter . . . is the one human expression of the identity of opposites," and "if we [']pataphysicians often feel our limbs shaken by laughter, it's the dreadful laughter from facing the clear evidence . . . that all defined existence is a scandal" ([1970] 1995, 28– 29). Bosse-de-Nage, the laughing subhuman, is a voice for such a syzygy. His "tautological monosyllable," *ha ha,* is a laugh track for the sophistry of *différance,* the limit between differing and deferring: "the two A's differ in space, when we write them, if not indeed in time, just as two twins are never born together" (Jarry [1911] 1965, 228). Not simply "A juxtaposed to A," but "A = A," the syzygy of such a guffaw is paradoxically both different and equivalent: "[p]ronounced slowly, it is the idea of duality," but "[p]ronounced quickly . . . it is the idea of unity" (228).

Bosse-de-Nage responds to the absurdity of ambiguity, dramatizing the *syzygia* of physics in a universe of undecidable uncertainty.[11] Quantum theories of symmetricality and reversibility almost seem to suggest that such a reality tests our mundane wits with its quantum puns. Each photon might be a point or a field. Each electron traveling forward through time might also be a positron traveling backward through time. Does not Faustroll propose a theory of gravity in which "the fall of a body towards a center" is the same as "the ascension of a vacuum towards a periphery" (Jarry [1911] 1965, 193)? Does not Sengle suggest that an infinitely smooth surface is indistinguishable from an infinitely rough surface (Jarry [1897] 1989, 105)? The *syzygia* simply ensures that such ambiguity is preserved in a world where we can no longer distinguish between reality and illusion.

Clinamen: The Principle of Deviance

Clinamen is the third declension of exception: the decline of the *swerve*. Detouring around every other thing in a system that values the fate of contrivance, it serves the will to digress. Jarry may borrow this notion from a classical context (the *clinamen* in Lucretius or even the *parenklisis* in Epicurus), but such a principle of deviance also provides a pretext for postmodern philosophy about the theme of misprision (e.g., the *détournement* in Derrida or the *déclination* in Serres)—vagaries that diverge from what directs them, escaping the events of the system that controls them. The *clinamen* is simply the unimpeded part of a flow which ensures that such a flow has no fate. Not unlike the spiral of Ubu or the vortex of Pound, such a swerve is the atomic glitch of a microcosmic incertitude—the symbol for a vital poetics, gone awry.

Lucretius writes that, "while the first bodies are being carried downwards by their own weight in a straight line through the void . . . , they swerve a little from their course" ([50 B.C.] 1975, 113), for without this uncertain swerve in space and time (*incerto tempore ferme incertisque locis*), "all would fall downwards like raindrops through the profound void, no collision would take place . . . : thus nature would never have produced anything" (113). The *clinamen* involves a Brownian kinetics, whose decline defies inertia since such a swerve must imply a change in vector without a change in force. The *clinamen* represents the minimal obliquity within a laminar trajectory. The curve is a tangent to a descent, but a tangent that defies all calculus since the curve is itself a tangent composed of nothing but tangents ad infinitum—the volute rhythm of a fractal contour.

Lucretius resorts to such a swerve in order to posit a choice between what Serres regards as two genres of physics: "Venus, that is to say, nature; or Mars, that is to say, nature" (Serres [1977] 1982a, 98). Venus denotes the eroticism of a nomad paralogy, the *voluptas* of a fluid dynamics (fold and flow), whereas Mars denotes the necrotism of a royal paradigm, the *voluntas* of a solid mechanics (rank and file).[12] Science has usually adopted the latter physics,[13] insofar as it murders to dissect, declaring martial law on behalf of whatever is repeatable and therefore predictable—the *foederi fati* of a terroristic determinism. Derrida implies, however, that the *clinamen* deflects this mandatory destiny into an aleatory ecstasy: "[t]he *clinamen* of the elementary principle . . . would be the pleasure principle" (1984, 8) — a libidinal rebellion: artfulness disrupting lawfulness.

Serres argues that, for such modern physics, "[t]he *clinamen* is a principal element of homeorrhesis," not of homeostasis ([1977] 1982a, 119). Atomic events do not *be* so much as *become:* their equilibrium does not repeat so much as change. Even though "the time of the *clinamen* is not necessarily simultaneous with leaving the dead to bury the dead" (99), such a swerve does provide a nomad cognate to the royal concept of entropy, be it in a flow of heat (as defined by Boltzmann) or in a flow of data (as defined by Shannon). Just as Lucretius draws an analogy between atoms and words, arguing that both substance and utterance result from a random complex of combinations and permutations (175), so also does Serres draw an analogy between thermionics and cybernetics, arguing that both sciences theorize the *clinamen* as either decay or noise.

Serres explains that, for Lucretius, any compound, be it chemical or syllabic, results from an aleatory act that in turn mistakes itself ex post facto as the result of a mandatory law: for example, "[t]he alphabetical proto-cloud is without law and the letters are scattered at random, always there as a set in space, as language; but as soon as a text or speech appears, the laws of good formulation, combination, and conjugation also appear ([1977] 1982a, 114).[14] No lawfulness can exist without such repetition of compounds; however, the *clinamen* serves to interject turbulence into the reprise of such lawful cycles in order to disrupt the *flow of influence* from cause to effect. As Derrida implies, such a swerve evokes the very "*atomystique* of the letter" (1984, 10), its portmanteau of quantum pulsion and lingual turmoil, both of which are ramified by poetry, if not unified by science.

McCaffery dramatizes such an *atomystique* by deploying the *clinamen* as a semantic strategy in his essay on the 'pataphysics of Zarathustra. Just as Lucretius argues that only the *clinamen* of a minimal errancy divides the fire (*ignes*) from the firs (*ligna*), so also does McCaffery transpose letters, inserting them or replacing them, doing so in order to divert the flow of his text with each typo. The increasing frequency of such miscreance eventually results in a display of cacophasia so that, for example, the word "*clinamen*" might become "chinamen" or "cinnamen" (1997, 16). For Jarry, the wordplay of such deviance often takes the form of the portmanteau (e.g., *cornegidouille* or *palcontentes*) — words that do not abbreviate or congregate two meanings so much as complicate their sequencing through an act of misprision that parodies their linguistic precedents.

Bloom argues that, because such misprision allows a poet to evade influence and become anomalous, "the study of Poetic Influence is necessarily a branch of 'Pataphysics" (1973, 42). Influence is no longer an interreference but an interference, in which divertissement replaces ressentiment. Precedent norms no longer inhibit subsequent forms since "the *clinamen* stems always from a 'pataphysical sense of the arbitrary" — the "equal haphazardness" of cause and effect: " '[p]ataphysics proves to be truly accurate; in the world of poets all irregularities are indeed 'regular exceptions'; the *recurrence* of vision is itself a law governing exceptions" (42). What repeats is not a rule of repetition and imitation but a game of competition and agitation, in which the *clinamen* is the smallest possible aberration that can make the greatest possible difference.

The Imaginary Solution

'Pataphysics misreads metaphysics in order to disrupt it, confuse it, or deflect it, transposing the relationship between a royal paradigm and a nomad paralogy until such a philosophy of exceptions goes even so far as to misread itself. Subsequent 'pataphysicians (the Italian Futurists, the French Oulipians, and the Canadian Jarryites) reinterpret their antecedent practitioners, misreading them in order to avoid the normalization of such abnormalities. Each predecessor is (mis)interpreted as a problem requiring a solution. As Bloom observes, "[t]his sense is *not reductive,* for it is the continuum, the stationing context, that is reseen, and shaped into the visionary; it is brought up to the intensity of the crucial objects, which then 'fade' into it" (1973, 42). In essence, each solution is itself the catalyst for a phantasm that in turn becomes a problem.

'Pataphysics may be a science of imaginary solutions, but this imaginariness does not entail its insignificance because, as McCaffery argues, "[t]hat the problem is a pseudo-problem in no way nullifies the pursuit of a solution for the pursuit in itself will evince the problematic nature of both 'problem' and 'solution' (1986, 189). Deleuze argues that a problem does not simply mean the failure of a theorem, whose ineptitude or incertitude can vanish through cumulative knowledge; instead, "[s]olutions are engendered at precisely the same time that the problem determines *itself*" ([1969] 1990, 121). Questions always define in advance the regime of their answers. The problem always persists in the very paradigm that allows the solution to make sense as a solution. No enigma is solved so well that its status as an enigma ceases to exist. A solution is infinitely imaginary.

'Pataphysics implies that all problems threaten to operate at the infinite disposal of a futile inquest. Baudrillard goes so far as to suggest that the object (with its fatal strategies of fascination) may pose a problem without solution for the subject (and its banal strategies of explanation) since attempts by science to render reality more explicable and controllable always threaten to render reality even more inexplicable and uncontrollable ([1987] 1988, 89). Science gazes at a crystal that promises to answer all questions but that instead captures science with a demand for even more questions. Like the evil genie feared by Descartes or the free spirit loved by Nietzsche, the crystal takes revenge upon the will to truth. The subject tries to *solve* the object, but meanwhile the object tries to *dissolve* the subject, and ultimately the object always triumphs.[15]

'Pataphysics effectively reveals that this demand for truth is only an imaginary solution to the deceit of such an object. Nietzsche asks: " 'Why do you not want to deceive?' especially if it should seem—and it does seem!—as if life aimed at . . . deception, simulation, delusion" ([1882] 1974, 281–82). Why believe in truth? Why not believe in untruth? Why does belief in either case take itself so seriously? Why does belief in effect believe in itself? Why not move from the deceit of truth to the truth of deceit? The science of 'pataphysics suggests that, without the mendacity of poetry, what the veracity of science reveals about the *horror vacui* of the universe, the fact that delusions are integral to all knowledge must seem utterly nightmarish. The value of poetry thus resides in its ability to play in this void that the truth of science must find in the real.

[A]utomatism always embodies an irrational projection of consciousness.
... There is a complete [']pataphysics of the object awaiting description
here, a science of imaginary technical solutions.
—Baudrillard [1968] 1996b, 113

[T]he unforeseen beast Clinamen ejaculated onto the walls of its universe.
—Jarry [1911] 1965, 238

3. Italian Futurism
A 'Pataphysics of Machinic Exception

The Machinic Future of Poetry

Italian Futurists present the first case for the surrationalism of the 'pataphysical, revising the structure of exception in order to oppose the irrationalism of the French symbolists. Futurism responds to the avant-garde pseudoscience of Jarry by inflecting the machinic intensities of technological forms, arguing that exception results from the collision of machines. For Marinetti, Futurism begins accidentally with such a mechanical catastrophe: a car wreck that dramatizes the *clinamen* of a swerve, complete with the anomalous intensity of its shock (*la scossa*), its noise (*il rumore*), and its speed (*la velocità*). Such an event implies that, from any havoc wreaked by technology, there appears a route charted for aesthetics. Such a 'pataphysical epistemology values the uniqueness, if not the randomness, of surprise itself.

Marinetti aligns Futurism with the modern advent of a cyborganic philosophy, in which an industry for hybridizing the anthropic and the machinic might parallel an artistry for hybridizing the poetic and the noetic: "[w]e cooperate with Mechanics in destroying the old poetry" ([1911] 1991, 75) since "[w]e want to make literature out of the life of a motor" ([1916] 1991, 95) — "[t]o listen to motors and to reproduce their conversations" (96). Futurism simply resorts to the metaphor *of the machine* in order to depict metaphor *as a machine,* arguing that, since "[n]othing is more beautiful

47

than a great humming central electric station . . . , panels bristling with dials, keyboards, and shining commutators," literature must learn to embrace the novelty of such technological modernization: "[t]hese panels are our only models for the writing of poetry" ([1914] 1991, 106).

Metaphor quite literally becomes a literary device, a mechanical conveyance, whose meaning descends etymologically (if not metaphorically) from the concept of vehicle, as the Greek word *metapherein*, "to transport," seems to suggest. When Marinetti claims that "a roaring car . . . is more beautiful than the *Victory of Samothrace*" ([1909] 1991, 49), he begins to literalize this metaphorical equivalence between the artistry of a message and the industry of its transit. If Futurism is the science that unleashes the accidental potentials of such machinic novelty, does not Futurism resemble the science by which Ubu might detonate his mechanized automatons, the Palcontents? Is it not possible to say in the spirit of Jarry that " '[p]ataphysics is the science of these present or future beings and devices, along with the power to use them" ([1894] 1965, 113)?

Futurism transforms 'pataphysics into an *applied science*, whose structure of exception has informed two kinds of radical politics (be it Italian Fascism or Russian Communism), both of which have responded poetically to the machinery of industrial capitalism by trying to imagine a reversible transition from a poetry *about* science to a science *of* poetry. This survey discusses such a sequence of influence according to the metaphor of the *accident*, the structure of an exception, in which the instruments of a royal science are inadvertently set free by the experiments of a nomad science (like the kind of extravagant speculation seen later, for example, in the junk metamatics of Tinguely or the auto collisions of Ballard): delirious machinery that revises the *anomalos*, the *syzygia*, and the *clinamen* through its own machinic paralogy of shock, noise, and speed.

Futurism versus Symbolism

Marinetti drives an automobile recklessly in order to declare that poetry must surrender itself to the Unknown: "[such] words were scarcely out of my mouth when I spun my car around . . . , and there, suddenly, were two cyclists coming toward me, shaking their fists, wobbling like two equally convincing but nevertheless contradictory arguments" ([1909] 1991, 48). The cyclists pose a "stupid dilemma" (48), requiring the motorist to swerve away from them into a ditch—an abject locale, where the poet in euphoria proclaims a manifesto in favor of such disasters. The car crash provides an allegory for an exorbitant spectacle of avoidance, in which every poetic device must act like an updated machine (a roadster) that veers away from the passéism of an outdated vehicle (a bicycle): "[p]oetry must be conceived as a violent attack on unknown forces" (49).

Marinetti invokes the tropes of Jarry in order to fuse science with poetry, but ironically enough, Jarry is himself a notorious cyclist, who portrays a pair of supermen on bicycles: Christ racing uphill against a velocipede toward a crucifixion ([1911] 1965, 124) and Marceuil racing overland against a locomotive toward an electrocution ([1902] 1964, 79). Marinetti seems to swerve from the path of such cyclists, as if to deploy the 'pataphysics of Jarry in order to parody the 'pataphysics of Jarry. Marinetti in effect dramatizes the principle of Bloom that 'pataphysics is itself a science of influence, insofar as Futurism must reverse the flow of cause and effect, denouncing the nostalgia for a prototype in order to replace it with the prognosis of an ectype. An antecedent device (the Futurist automobile) must evade the obstacle of a precedent device (the Symbolist velocipede).

Burliuk has observed that, despite such antagonism, "[e]very Symbolist has a Futurist tucked under his arm" ([1915] 1988, 96) — particularly when we take into account that Jarry (a friend to Symbolists) does indeed inspire Marinetti (an enemy to Symbolists). Both Futurism and Symbolism do criticize science 'pataphysically by proposing a synaesthetic transvaluation of rationalism, but Marinetti must nevertheless insist upon staging a duel (if not a race) between Futurism and Symbolism, given that he plays a game of chicken to see which artist, which driver, first loses the nerve to enact a collision between two different categories of *vehicle* that can convey poetic tropes. Marinetti values the sport of such a conflict, in which his respect for a 'pataphysical precursor at the same time clashes with his disdain for a 'pataphysical precursor.

Marinetti proclaims that "[w]e have even dreamed of one day being able to create a mechanical son, the fruit of pure will, a synthesis of all the laws that science is on the brink of discovering" ([1911] 1991, 83). Evoking the story of *Frankenstein,* in which the creator (a prototype) and the monster (an ectype) transpose their roles through a precession of simulacra, Futurism strives to imagine its own brand of celibate creation. Whereas Jarry is perhaps the kind of robot child that Marinetti wishes to father, Jarry is in fact the father of the robot child that Marinetti is. As Jarry observes, "[t]he Machine is born of the ashes of the slave" ([1894] 1965, 112). Like a dangerous supplement, every machinic tool augments, then replaces, the anthropic limb that wields it. Each limb that constructs a prosthesis for itself risks not self-emendation but self-amputation.

Marinetti demands that this hybrid device of machinic metaphors must forge the industries of tomorrow to abolish the forgeries of yesterday. Futurism must practice a "hygienic forgetfulness" ([1911] 1991, 105) that amounts to a literal *breaking of records* (in both senses of the term), destroying not only standards for performance but also histories of performance, not only ascending past a limit (with ever more energy) but also rescinding the limit that is the past (with ever less memory). Futurism disavows the passéism of an obsolete technique for the sake of a synchronistic disappearance, advocating the destruction of museums, for example, on the assumption that they are nothing more than the "absurd abattoirs of painters and sculptors ferociously macerating each other with color-blows and line-blows, the length of the fought-over walls" (Marinetti [1909] 1991, 49).

Futurism in effect aspires to imitate the machinic graffiti of Faustroll, who devastates a museum with "the Painting Machine," a revolving gyroscope that whirls at random through "the Palace of Machines," mechanically vandalizing masterpieces: "it dashed itself against the pillars, swayed and veered in infinitely varied directions, and followed its own whim in blowing onto the walls' canvas the succession of primary colors ranged according to the tubes of its stomach" ([1911] 1965, 238). The Painting Machine (which actually bears the name *Clinamen*) prefigures the 'pataphysical technologies of Tinguely (particularly the metamatic entitled *Homage to New York,* a calliope for painting pictures at random while destroying itself inside the Museum of Modern Art). Such a device swerves through an aesthetic tradition, wreaking havoc upon its artifacts.

Tinguely builds devices that fuse the detritus of both artistry and industry into an assemblage of incompatible accessories, all of which sabotage their own instrumentality (as if to suggest that, like a 'pataphysical science, such a technological machine generates itself from excess debris used capriciously and incompatibly to generate more excess debris).[1] What Tinguely regards as a "joyful" machine (Hulten 1987, 56) is merely the product of what Nietzsche regards as a "joyful" science. The machinic delirium of such epistemic vandalism signifies a competition between poetic tropes that collide and collude in order to create the *clinamen* of an artistic accident— an event that sets free each part of the device itself (including its user). As Tinguely might claim, such a "machine is . . . an instrument that allows me to be poetic" (Hulten 1987, 56).

Fascism versus Communism

Shershenevich observes that "[t]he Futurists do not take you 'to,' but 'from' " so that "the cannonball, once fired, gets wild and describes a curve (excesses . . .)," its detours always leading away from the capitalistic philistinism of the bourgeoisie ([1916] 1988, 153–54). Whether Italian or Russian, both pedigrees of Futurism have reacted 'pataphysically to the age of industrial automation by divorcing the project of science from the program of capital, doing so through the politics of either Fascism or Communism (even though both of these political movements have generally dismissed Futurism in favor of a bourgeois aesthetic: realism itself). Like the Painting Machine, Futurism unleashes uncontrollable potentialities, waging a random battle in which a subaltern science of experimental reason subverts a dominant science of instrumental reason.

Careening through the archive of history, the *clinamen* of 'pataphysics precipitates a cyclical reversal of influence so that, as Khlebnikov might argue, "science is now following the path that language has already taken" ([1919] 1987, 378). Poetry inspires a scientific endeavor that poetry in turn becomes. Just as Jarry inspires Marinetti (whose poetry evades a French precursor), so also do the Italian Futurists inspire the Russian Futurists (whose poetry evades an Italian precursor); moreover, the Russian Futurists go on to inspire the Russian Formalists (whose science is based upon a Futurist precursor), just as the Russian Formalists go on to inspire the French Structuralists (whose science is based upon a Formalist precursor). For Futurism, these ironic cycles of recursive influence merely comprise an evasive history of warfare without any unilinear intention.

Marinetti claims that such warfare is itself "Futurism intensified" ([1916] 1991, 131)—perhaps because (as Deleuze and Guattari might suggest), war is the *supplement* of a marginal episteme, occurring wherever a royal science clashes with a nomad science ([1980] 1987, 355): the former, building *implements* (which control energy through instrumental *tasks*); the latter, building *armaments* (which unleash energy through experimental *risks*).[2] While Benjamin argues that, for such radical warfare, "alienation has reached such a degree that it can experience its own destruction as an aesthetic pleasure" ([1936] 1969, 242), the very aesthetic that has served what he vilifies (Fascism) has at the same time served what he endorses (Communism). More hyperbolic than antonymic in its logic, Futurism counteracts the atrocity of capitalist automation with an even greater atrocity. Heidegger observes that the millenary problem of technology, the danger of the *Gestell* ([1962] 1977,

42), always already involves an imaginary solution *through* technology: that is, every problem implies a fateful paradox, since the solution to such a problem is itself *a problem of the problem*.[3] The potential for a transition from danger to safety stems from the insight of a *clinamen*, a turning away that is itself an *Einkehr*, an "in-turning," if not an *Einblitz*, an "in-flashing" (41): "[p]erhaps we stand already in the shadow cast ahead by the advent of *this* turning" — "[w]hen and how it [comes] to pass after the manner of a destining no one knows" (41) because "[t]he turning of the danger comes to pass suddenly" (44) — as if by accident. 'Pataphysics studies the exception of such accidents (in order to *traffic* in the secret order of their conceits).

'Pataphysics regards the insight, the *Einblitz*, of such accidents as a collision between two alien orders that compare their disparate events and exchange their desperate images in a mutual clash of misprision. For Marinetti, the accident of such a *clinamen* becomes a dynamic synonym for an epiphany, an *Einkehr*, that contributes to the cataclysm of a self-propelled self—the *automobility*, not only of a device, but also of its driver. For Marinetti, the car crash that gives birth to Futurism merely enacts the anomalous intensity of such an insight by providing the basis in the future for an imaginary philosophy of 'pataphysical speculations. As Deleuze and Guattari suggest, "*there are itinerant, ambulant sciences that consist in following a flow in a vectorial field across which singularities are scattered like so many 'accidents'* (problems)" ([1980] 1987, 372).

Paradigms in Collision

Ballard in *Crash* has extended this 'pataphysical speculation of Marinetti to its most baroque extreme by imagining a future science in which accidents reveal a portent about the exceptional spontaneity of every poetic device. Ballard dissects automobile collisions with the clinical attitude of a surgeon, depicting the crash test as a kind of sadoerotic foreplay for the intense orgasms of the victim and the voyeur (both of whom copulate in an imaginary porno film — a movie eventually made real by Cronenberg).[4] For Baudrillard, the vehicle of metaphor in such a text succumbs, like a roadster, to the destiny of the accident — following "a path leading more quickly than the main road, or leading where the main road does not lead or, better yet, and to parody Littré in a [']pataphysical mode, 'a path leading nowhere, but leading there faster than the others' " ([1981] 1994b, 118).

Baudrillard observes that, in *Crash*, "the Accident is everywhere" since "[i]t is no longer the exception to a triumphal rationality, it has become the

Rule, it has devoured the Rule" — "[i]t is no longer even the 'accursed share,' the one conceded to destiny by the system itself"; instead, "[e]verything is reversed" ([1981] 1994b, 113). The accident reveals a 'pataphysical promiscuity between any two uncorrelated occurrences — their uncanny ability to collide on a whim into a potential infinity of exceptional permutations: "[i]t is the Accident that gives form to life, it is the Accident . . . that *is the sex of life*" (113). The accident is "[t]he only strategy . . . of [']pataphysics . . . ; that is, a science-fiction of the system's reversal against itself at the extreme limit of simulation, a reversible simulation in a hyperlogic of . . . destruction" ([1976] 1993a, 4–5).

Ballard suggests that every vehicular collision reveals a coincidental synchronicity in which unrelated incidents relate to each other as if in a poetic milieu: for example, "Christ's crucifixion could be regarded as the first traffic accident — certainly if we accept Jarry's happy piece of anticlericalism" ([1969] 1990, 25), which compares the Golgotha (with its stations of the crucifix) to a velodrome (with its pit stops for a bicycle). Jarry subjects the Passion to a *clinamen,* equating the death of Jesus Christ with a "deplorable accident" in a bike race ([1911] 1965, 124), just as Ballard subjects this story by Jarry to a *clinamen,* equating the death of John F. Kennedy with a "deplorable incident" in an auto race ([1969] 1990, 108): "Jesus . . . had a flat right away" when "Pilate gave the send-off" (Jarry [1911] 1965, 122); likewise, "Kennedy got off to a bad start" when "Oswald was the starter" (Ballard 1990, 108).

Jarry and Ballard in both cases depict death itself as the outcome of a traffic violation, and this thematic parallel between the two writers almost seems to dramatize their interest in coincidence itself. Like Jarry, Ballard tells a 'pataphysical story that swerves away from a metaphysical history, but like Marinetti, Ballard also tells a 'pataphysical story that swerves away from a 'pataphysical history. Both kinds of swerve involve the sudden excursion away from the influential through an execution of the influential — the regicide, so to speak, of a king by a poet. What Futurism regards as the hygiene of warfare refers to this conflict in the anxiety of influence — a conflict in which the poet stages a militant accident, pitting a new rule of the now against the old rule of the law.

Futurism resorts to the *clinamen* of such accidental collisions in order to divert the anxiety of influence into the ecstasy of exception. Such a *clinamen* transforms the Oedipal metaphysics of ressentiment into the non-Oedipal 'pataphysics of divertissement. The Oedipal subject is atomized and dispersed in a traject rather than localized and coalesced around an object.

The royal monument of the ego merges with the nomad movement of a car so that, in effect, the auto of the self is propelled into its own drives. The *clinamen* of this subjective dispersion evokes a cyborganic schizonoia[5] — what Marinetti might call *fisicofollia,* or "body-madness" ([1915] 1991, 128), the ecstasy of a 'pataphysician, for whom "[t]his new drama of Futurist surprise and geometric splendor is a thousand times more interesting . . . than human psychology" ([1914] 1991, 106).

Marinetti equates the force of industrial automation with the violent desires of the unconscious itself — the ecstasy of a machinic accident that has come to dramatize the *syzygia* of both the erotic and the necrotic: "motors, they say, are truly mysterious" for "[t]hey have whims, freakish impulses" ([1914] 1991, 99), expressing the kind of libidinal intensity seen, for example, in the autoerotic accidents described by Ballard. Futurism imagines an impossible technology in which every device is a sex toy that can destroy thought itself (not unlike *les machines malthusiennes* of Jarry or *les machines célibataires* of Duchamp). What such 'pataphysicians have called "bachelor machines," Deleuze and Guattari have called "desiring-machines" ([1972] 1983, 1) — deviant devices whose extravagance evokes all the ecstatic tortures of shock, noise, and speed.

The Shock of Exception

Carrouges suggests that "[a] *bachelor machine is first of all an improbable machine*" (1975, 21), an apparatus of anomalies: "[e]very bachelor machine is first of all a [']pataphysical machine, or a patamachine" (44). Such an apparatus does not repeat any model of the erotic in which the erotic becomes a means to repeat: "the bachelor machine is the erotic form of malthusianism" insofar as the device perverts the values of functional repetition, opposing all forms of love that provide an alibi for replicative engineering. Whether electric or artistic, the shock (*la scossa*) generated by such a device short-circuits the laws that forbid perpetual motion and libidinal action. The bachelor machines inflict the shock of a nomad science upon the mastery of devices: the royal mandate not only to construct a machine but also to determine its purpose.

Duchamp has provided the seminal pretext for such a machine in his vitreal diptych, *The Bride Stripped Bare by Her Bachelors, Even* — a window through which voyeurs might witness a sadoerotic collision, postponed in the hyperspace of an alternate dimension: the upper panel depicting the Bride (built from Draft Pistons fueled by the combustion of an ecstatic gasoline); the lower panel depicting the Bachelors (built from Malic Moulds attached to an array of diverse devices: a Water Wheel, a Chocolate Grinder, a Butterfly Pump, etc.). Jerry-rigged from Jarry-rigged ideas, this blueprint of schizoid gadgetry dramatizes the shock of coincidental correlations (the *clinamen* of which is only highlighted by the fact that the glass itself has since become riven with cracks—the result of a jolt suffered during vehicular transport).

Anastasi suggests that Duchamp uses this machine to perform a *clinamen* upon the devices of Jarry. Just as Jarry deploys the electric chair of *The Supermale* in order to imagine a pseudoscience of perpetual motion, so also does Duchamp resort to the electric motor of *The Bachelors* in order to imagine a pseudoscience of libidinal action—the *as if* of what Duchamp might call a science of *hypophysics* (Anastasi 1991, 88). Such a science permits Duchamp to regard each of his own impossible hypotheses as an otherwise imaginable condition that has merely become detached from the alternate dimension of its own possibility: "I was interested in introducing [into my work] the precise . . . aspect of science," but "[i]t wasn't for love of science that I did this; on the contrary, it was rather in order to discredit it, mildly, lightly, unimportantly" ([1967] 1971, 39).

Carrouges has suggested that such a science plots the fantastic inversion of an Oedipal dynamic, since the Bride, not the Bachelor, acts as a sado-erotic superego that tortures a masochist id (1954, 45); however, Szeemann observes that "the Bachelor Machine . . . as suggested by Carrouges [has] in part been vehemently rejected by the 'pataphysicians on account of the 'upper inscription' which exerts an influence on the Bachelors and determines their fate" (1975, 11). Carrouges still deploys an Oedipal paradigm to describe what Deleuze and Guattari insist is a non-Oedipal artifice: "[a] genuine consummation is achieved by the new machine, a pleasure that can be rightly called autoerotic, or rather automatic: the nuptial celebration of a new alliance, a new birth . . . , as though the eroticism of the machine liberated other unlimited forces" ([1972] 1983, 18).[6]

Bachelor machines amplify *la scossa* of sensation to a null point of synaesthetic indifference where any hierarchy of experience, be it torture or ecstasy, disappears altogether, giving rise instead to an infinitive series of positive traits that never express a definitive system with negative values. Machines with such freedom never have to prove their ability, since they fulfill no real purpose, no true command. For this reason, Brock suggests that such 'pataphysical instruments constitute the machinic solution to a chimerical problem: they are "*mental machines,* the imaginary working of which suffices to produce a real movement of the mind" (1975, 44), and "[t]o operate the world of Bachelor Machines means taking the world only as we perceive it" (81), regarding reality not as a metaphysical substance but as a 'pataphysical surface: a (dis)simulation.

Certeau suggests that, within such a paralogy, bachelor machines perform their ecstatic tortures not upon a victim so much as upon a medium, the shocking violence acted out not semantically beyond language but syntactically within language (1975, 88)—against the very machinery of language, challenging the productive capacity of this machine to display the world of the *as is,* while emphasizing the seductive capacity of this machine to invent a world of the *as if.* Lyotard makes a similar argument when he claims that the bachelor machine inhabits an imaginary dimension of dissimulating machinations, providing the basis for a sophistic alternate to metaphysics itself: "we have to choose which camp to be in, as did . . . Jarry . . . and Nietzsche: the Sophists against the Philosophers, . . . the Bachelor machines against industrial mechanics" ([1977] 1990, 49).

Lyotard argues that such a device does not exploit nature through a use (as gadgetry does) nor does such a device destroy nature through a war (as weaponry does); instead, such a device entraps nature through an art—the deception of simulation:[7] "it plays a *trick* on these forces, being itself less strong than they are, and making real this monstrosity: that the less strong [must] be stronger than what is stronger" ([1977] 1990, 42). The word "machine," in fact, stems from the Latin word *machina,* meaning "trickery"— a device to deceive, as if the machine reveals that for the *as if,* all orders are invertible and all series are reversible: "[t]o every discourse there must be another opposing it in a rigourously parallel manner, but leading to the opposite conclusion: sophistics is above all the art of making these . . . duplicitous speeches, *dissoi logoi*" (47).[8]

Marinetti demands that such a poetic wisdom create the kind of "matter whose essence must be grasped by strokes of intuition, the kind of thing that the physicists and chemists can never do" ([1916] 1991, 95) because, "[d]espite the most skillful deformations, the syntactic sentence always contains a scientific . . . perspective absolutely contrary to the . . . emotional perspective" ([1911] 1991, 108). Science has traditionally resorted to a syntax of reason, in which the literary line of poetry must become the assembly line of science, but Futurism renounces this linear syntax for the sake of a "free speech" (*le parole in libertà*) that no longer serves this industrial mechanics. Such an imagination without puppet strings (*l'immaginazione senza fili*) no longer follows the "wire" of syntax but instead mimics the noise of radio static as transmitted by a wireless gone haywire.[9]

The Noise of Exception

Deleuze and Guattari argue that, because "[d]esiring-machines work only when they break down, and by continually breaking down" ([1972] 1983, 8), such machines always constitute a system of interruptions in which every component behaves like a *clinamen:* "[e]very machine functions as a break in the flow in relation to the machine to which it is connected, but at the same time is also a flow itself . . . in relation to the machine connected to it" (36). What Deleuze and Guattari define in terms of mechanical disruption, Serres might define in terms of a cyborganic parasitism, since both concepts signify a "noisiness" whose interferent perturbance not only subverts the redundancy but also enriches the complexity of any system (be it the mathetic codes of computers, the semiotic codes of societies, or even the biologic codes of organisms).[10]

Serres deploys such tropes in his own effort to insist that, ultimately, "[n]oise is the basic element of the software of all our logic" ([1982] 1995, 7). Noise is intrinsic to every system that regards it as extrinsic to its own system: in other words, "science is its own *noise* with itself, it produces its noise from itself" (136), doing so until it cannot hear its own noise, let alone its own words, because of all the noise that it makes through the controversies of its contradiction: "noise . . . is at the boundaries of physics, and physics is bathed in it" (13–14). Noise provides a metaphor for the *as if* of all that is possible yet unthought.[11] It denotes the *Traumwelt* of a *(para)site*— a marginal location where a nomad science attacks a royal science: there, a machinic praxis always arises, as if by chance, from a machinic parapraxis.

Futurism values such mechanized parasitism, insofar as Marinetti argues that just as "[m]icrobes . . . are essential to the health of the intestines," so also is there "a microbe essential to the vitality of *art*" ([1914] 1991, 97). Futurism equates this microbe with the parasite of a *clinamen*—the 'pataphysical turbulence of noise (*il rumore*). Unlike metaphysics, which values music, not noise, in the syntax of reason, 'pataphysics inverts this system of values, equating *il rumore* with the novelty of anomaly—hence, we see the use of onomatopocia in the poetry of Marinetti, who mimics the kind of symphonic cacophony that Russolo, the Futurist composer, evokes with his own *intonarumori:* "machines create today such a large number of varied noises that pure sound, with its littleness and its monotony, now fails to arouse any emotion" ([1913] 1967, 5).

Marinetti attempts to arouse such emotion with an automated invective that abolishes standard grammar in order to evoke the "zang-tuuum tuuumb orchestra of the noises of war swelling with anger under a note of silence" ([1914] 1987, 79). Just as Marinetti privileges telegrammatic abbreviations enhanced by such sound effects as "2000 steam pregnancies *tataploomploom flac* flac" (63), so also does Russolo replace the antiquated repertoire of symphonic sonograms with "the rumblings and rattlings of engines breathing . . . , the rising and falling of pistons, the stridency of mechanical saws" ([1913] 1967, 8). Such noise is more surrational than irrational, providing the basis for what Khlebnikov might call the *zaum* of a "transrational" language (the *zaumnyi iazyk*)—not nonsense, but "beyonsense"—a "language situated beyond the boundaries of ordinary reason" ([1919] 1987, 383).

Khlebnikov suggests that, for science, the noisiness of *zaum* can no longer be dismissed as an exceptional irrelevance: "[t]he plenitude of language must be analyzed in terms of fundamental units of 'alphabetic verities,' and then for these sound elements we may be able to construct something resembling Mendeleev's law or Moseley's law—the latest achievements of the science of chemistry" ([1919] 1987, 376). Like *il rumore* of Italian Futurism, the *zaum* of Russian Futurism not only attempts to disrupt the basis for a royal science of the past but also attempts to provide the basis for a nomad science of the future. *Zaum* in effect attempts to transmit the noise, *il rumore,* of the bachelor machines in order to produce a concomitant 'pataphysics for such linguistic technology. What is noise in the paradigm of nostalgia is music to the prognosis of paralogy.

Tynyanov observes that the *zaum* of Russian Futurists might provide the poetic foundation for the noetic enterprise of the Russian Formalists (who resort to such poetry for examples of concepts that science might deploy in the study of poetry itself) ([1928] 1979, 153). Formalism almost verges upon the 'pataphysical insofar as its scientific evaluation of poetry privileges the novelty of anomaly—the surprising noises in the alienation effect of *ostranenie.* Like Futurism, such Formalism tries to use the language of scientific methodology in order to examine the neglected machinery of language itself, not the word as sign but the word as such (*slovo kak takovoe*). Such a machine embodies a 'pataphysical retroversion that does not simply use its devices to convey a narrative meaning but uses such meaning as an excuse to deploy innovative devices.

Tynyanov almost appears to advocate a 'pataphysical literariness when he suggests that "if new phenomena are to emerge in literature, what is needed is relentless intellectual activity, and belief in it, together with the scientific processing of material—even if such work is unacceptable to science" ([1878] 1979, 153). Tynyanov observes that Khlebnikov often resorts to the *clinamen* of a scientific misprision to generate the novelty of poeticized exceptions: "[p]oetry is close to science in its methods—this is what Khlebnikov teaches" (153) — "[m]inor mistakes, 'chance features,' explained by the old academics as a deviation caused by incomplete experimentation, serve as a catalyst for new discoveries: what was explained by 'incomplete experimentation' turns out to be the action of unknown laws" (150).

Tynyanov implies that "[p]oetry must be as open as science is in facing phenomena" so that "when it comes across a 'chance feature,' it must reorganise itself so that the chance feature ceases to be chance" ([1878] 1979, 154). Khlebnikov also argues that "[a] misprint, born involuntarily from the typesetter's will, suddenly gives meaning to a new entity; it is one of the forms of collective creativity and may thus be hailed as a desirable assistance to the artist" ([1919] 1987, 381–82). Such a *clinamen* draws attention to the material nature of the letter, revealing, for example, a 'pataphysical resemblance between syntax and optics in the letter Z, a letter depicting "the equality of the angle of incidence to the angle of reflection" (Khlebnikov [1917] 1987, 338)—almost as if the *clinamen* of the letter is itself a flash of deviant insight whose tropes of deflection and refraction take place at the speed of light.

The Speed of Exception

Baudrillard observes that, for 'pataphysics, history escapes from the gravity of the real in order to experience what Virilio might call "dromomania" ([1976] 1986, 4)[12]—the ecstatic velocity of simulation. Marinetti dramatizes such a millennial principle of 'pataphysics, when he exalts *la velocità* of the *clinamen* and the high-speed collision of bachelor machines: "[o]ne must kneel before the whirling speed of a gyroscope compass: 20,000 revolutions per minute" ([1911] 1991, 104); "[o]ne must snatch from the stars the secret [that might] let us match their speeds to escape from a greater star or to strike a smaller one" (104). The rotary engine of such a gyroscope calls to mind the physick-stick in Jarry or the turning-bar in Lyotard—devices that promise to break the second law of thermodynamics through an infinitized expenditure of energy.[13]

Jarry deploys the trope of such a *perpetuum mobile* in order to depict the allegorical competition between two genres of dromomanic technology: a bicycle team and an express train—the former representing the art of what Jarry might call "old cyclophile hagiographers" ([1911] 1965, 123); the latter representing the art of what Marinetti might call "the great Futurist Railroad" ([1909] 1991, 55). Such a race demonstrates the efficacy of Perpetual Motion Food, "a fuel for the human machine that [might] indefinitely delay . . . nervous fatigue, repairing it as it is spent" (Jarry [1900] 1964, 4). Such a race provides an allegory for the triumph of science over its own entropic necrosis. Just as the cyclist, who is a cadaver, can nevertheless pedal faster than ever despite having expired, so also does science represent a vertiginous expenditure that thrives paradoxically upon its own decline.

Jarry and Marinetti equate the *as if* of such a dromomanic technology with a scientific revolution whose history defies the royal order of causality itself. Inspired by Wells, for example, Jarry describes "[a] Machine to isolate us from Duration" ([1899] 1965, 115)—a time machine, whose three gyrostats rotate so fast that they immobilize the mechanism in the hyperspace of an alternate dimension. While Jarry may indulge in 'pataphysical speculations about the manufacture of such a bachelor machine, the device can exist only in the interzone of a surrational imagination. Such a device strives to provide imaginary solutions to its own problematic temporality. Just as Cubism depicts objects from several positions at once in order to defy the limits of space, so also does Futurism imagine objects from several momentums at once in order to defy the limits of time.

Wells observes that "[w]e cannot . . . appreciate this machine, any more than we can the spoke of a wheel spinning, or a bullet flying through the air," for "[i]f it is travelling through time . . . a hundred times faster than we are, if it gets through a minute while we get through a second, the impression it creates [must] of course be only . . . one-hundredth of what it . . . make[s] if it [is] not travelling in time" ([1895] 1987, 36–37). The time machine reduces history itself to a state of synchronistic disappearance (as if to suggest that, because kinesic realism relies upon periodic lapses of attention at a constant speed of movement, the world of existence arises only from our own persistence of vision). The time machine almost resembles a film machine, insofar as both kinds of device can depict plural instants of motion within a single picture of events.

Marinetti recognizes that the dromomania of such cinematic machinery can provide Futurism with "a prodigious sense of simultaneity and omnipresence" ([1917] 1991, 138). Cinema thus becomes the most poetically privileged genre of speed. Like Balla and Carrà, whose Futurist paintings almost resemble the chronophotography of Marey, Marinetti attempts to transform a diachronic sequence into a synchronic continuum, breaking the filmic syntax of a series, in order to perform the linguistic equivalent of a jump cut or a stop trick (as if *la velocità* itself can dematerialize the events of reality, producing a *syzygia,* each cause and its effect blurring together in the gyroscopic revolution of a physick-stick): "*this is how we decompose and recompose the universe according to our marvellous whims*" (142).[14]

Marinetti suggests that to be fast results in the "intuitive synthesis" of rectilinear forms (the prognosis of straight lines), whereas to be slow results in the "rational analysis" of curvilinear forms (the nostalgia of undulant lines) ([1914] 1991, 103). Blind to the fractals of tomorrow, Marinetti aligns the futurity of velocity with a royal genre of *mathesis:* he does not see that, while the extremes of *la velocità* may permit the future to outrace the past, such speed always risks the accident of a *clinamen,* in which a forward vector swerves into a backward vortex (particularly when we consider that, for quantum physics, even absolute speeds promise to diverge into an involute theory). If one travels very fast (but not above the limit of light), one travels into the future, but if one travels even faster (*beyond* the limit of light), one travels into the past.

Jarry argues that such time travel occurs only within the surreality of the *as if:* "the Machine can reach the real Past only after having passed through the Future," since "it must go through a point symmetrical to our Present, a dead center between future and past, and which can be designated precisely as the *Imaginary Present*" ([1899] 1965, 121). The Machine has *two pasts,* not only the one preceding its invention but also the one preceding its operation—which is to say, "the past *created by the Machine* when it returns to our Present and which is in effect the reversibility of the Future" (121). The "Futurism" of such 'pataphysics operates paradoxically in the tense of the *post modo,* the Futurist moving forward, forgetting the past, only by moving backward, revisiting the past, as if "[d]uration is the transformation of a succession into a reversion" (121).

Baudrillard suggests that, "[w]hen light is captured and swallowed by its own source, there is then a brutal involution of time into the event itself" ([1983] 1990a, 17). Such a singularity constitutes a "[c]atastrophe in the literal sense: the . . . curve that has its origin and end coincide in one . . . , yielding to an event without precedent and without consequences—[a] pure event," one whose reality disappears through a simulacral precession (17). 'Pataphysics suggests that "[s]peed itself is doubtless only this: throughout and beyond all technology, the temptation for things and people to go faster than their cause, to thereby catch up to their beginning and annul it" (162). Futurism is thus the effect of a paradoxical temporality in which Marinetti reverses his relation to Jarry so that 'pataphysics might originate in the future, not in the past.

The Chimeric Science of the Future

Futurism almost begins to propose for poetry the same kind of molecular revolution that Deleuze and Guattari later propose for science. Marinetti imagines a machinic paralogy that examines the unique specificity of matter and the absurd singularity of its events without resorting to anthropic prejudice: "[b]e careful not to force human feelings onto matter"; instead, "divine its different governing impulses, its forces of compression, dilation, cohesion, and disaggregation, its crowds of massed molecules and whirling electrons"; after all, "we are not interested in offering dramas of humanized matter" ([1916] 1991, 95). For such a dehumanized sensibility, the cyborganism of 'pataphysics must play itself out both *genetically* and *generically* so that any hybrid of the anthropic and the machinic parallels the hybrid of the poetic and the noetic.

Marinetti argues that "a strip of steel interests us for itself; that is, the . . . nonhuman alliance of its molecules or its electrons" ([1916] 1991, 95), and thus "[t]o the conception of the imperishable . . . , we oppose, in art, that of . . . the perishable, the transitory" ([1911] 1991, 75), since "matter has an admirable continuity of impulse toward . . . greater movement, a greater subdivision of itself" ([1916] 1991, 96).[15] Futurism subscribes to an atomist dynamic of *becoming* in which the machine does not represent the universe as a mechanismic assembly line of causes and effects (each event a *reprise* in the plan of its engineer); instead, such a machine represents the universe as a cyborganismic fracture plane of forces and energy (each event a *surprise* to the bias of its conjurer). The universe is simply a celibate creation for finding out what happens next: it is a surprise machine.

Marinetti hopes to evoke a molecular revolution that might take the 'pataphysical epistemology of Jarry by surprise, augmenting its declensions of exception through the machinic paralogy of shock, noise, and speed. Marinetti resorts to 'pataphysics in order to revise 'pataphysics, doing so in order to imagine the *as if* of a future in which poetry can instigate a science, whose "lyric equations" ([1914] 1991, 110) might in turn explain poetry itself. The Italian Futurists are among the first to posit such a grammatical algebra, just as the French Oulipians later posit their own procedural calculus (but whereas the Italian 'pataphysicians do so by referring to the *hardware* of a technological form and its concrete machines, the French pataphysicians do so by referring to the *software* of a numerological form and its abstract machines).

Futurism ultimately postulates an applied science of poetic theories, in which poetry itself is an accidental instrument for a scientific experiment. Rossiyansky observes that, in effect, Futurism dreams of "a future era . . . where scientific laboratories are run by astrologers and chiromantists" ([1913] 1988, 143) — 'pataphysical sophisters who parody metaphysical physicists. Graal-Arelsky observes in turn that, for Futurism, "[s]cience turns out to be relative, like everything else," since "[t]he world which rules in our intellect is not real, but imaginary" — as if reality itself emerges from a 'pataphysical perspectivism ([1912] 1988, 111). Such an avant-garde pseudoscience reveals that the Future is nothing more than a poetic notion that provides an absurd domain for the epistemic fantasies of 'pataphysics: the *as if* of its own science fiction.

That which certain writers have introduced with talent (even with genius)
in their work . . . , (Oulipo) intends to do systematically and scientifically,
if need be through recourse to machines that process information.

    —Oulipo [1973] 1986, 27

[D]ays are spooky . . . now that my dissertation is insane.

    —RACTER 1984, [36]

4. French Oulipianism

A 'Pataphysics of Mathetic Exception

Machinic Mathesis

French Oulipians present the second case for the surrationalism of the
'pataphysical, revising the structure of exception in order to oppose the
irrationalism of the French Surrealists. Members of Oulipo (*l'ouvroir de
littérature potentielle*)[1] respond to the avant-garde pseudoscience of Jarry
by inflecting the mathetic intensities of numerological forms, arguing that
exception results from the constraint of programs. Like Futurism, Oulipo
regards literature as a cyborganic phenomenon that results from deliberate
collisions between poetic devices: the machinic paralogy of accidents. For
the Oulipians, writing is automatic, insofar as it results not from an aleatory impulse (as in Surrealism) but from a mandatory purpose (as in Mannerism): writing is itself a machine to be studied methodically and guided
systematically, as if by a science.

Inspired by Jarry, Oulipo has revised the structure of exception by using
a 'pataphysical epistemology to study the *syzygia* between the *anomalos* of
a "constraint" and the *clinamen* of its "potentials." Working under the aus-
pices of a speculative institution (*le collège de 'pataphysique*), members of
Oulipo (who include, among others, such literati as Queneau, Lionnais,
Calvino, and Perec) study three unique species of exceptional eventuality:
the excess of order emerging out of chaos, the chiasm existing between order
and chaos, and the swerve of chaos breaking away from order. Such 'pata-

physics attempts to reconcile the dichotomy that metaphysics must establish between the *mathema* of a nomic, predetermined law (the *fata* of the *as is*) and the *poiesis* of a ludic, indeterminate art (the *alea* of the *as if*).

Oulipo resorts to 'pataphysics in order to suggest that even a machinic calculus has the potential to generate the novelty of anomaly. Just as science might propose rigorous systems for producing innovative knowledge, so also might poetry propose rigorous systems for producing innovative literature. Like the Futurists, who explore the molecularity of a machinic language, so also do the Oulipians resort to a lingual atomism in order to imagine their own anagrammatic radicalities. Such an axiomatic condition provides the basis for a 'pataphysical mathematics, whose ludic rules oppose the royal science of structural linguistics. Such a nomad science suggests that the mathesis of anagrams can subtend a cybernetic literature of the future (the potential of which has already been portended by such novelties as Web sites, hypertexts, and video games).

Oulipo explores the epistemology of this *potentiality,* replacing the metaphysics of thetical cases with the 'pataphysics of hypothetical cases—the *als ob,* the "as if," of what might have been. Like Futurism, Oulipo sees its work in terms of an as yet unrealized reality that exists paradoxically before its time and ahead of its time, taking place in the tense of the *post modo.* Such an avant-garde pseudoscience endeavors to create potential problems in the present so that writers in the future might provide an imaginary solution. Such a discipline functions within a ludic genre of speculative experiments: "Is there any other canonical way of viewing the future (whether one calls oneself serious in the . . . [']pataphysical sense of the word), than as a bouquet of Imaginary Solutions—that is, of potentialities?" (Oulipo [1983] 1986, 50).

The College of 'Pataphysics

Oulipo represents an auxiliary outgrowth of the College of 'Pataphysics —an absurd school, founded in 1948 in order to preserve the memory of Jarry by publishing *Cahiers* and *Dossiers* about his avant-garde pseudoscience. Reminiscent of the projectors from Lagado (as in the work of Swift) or even the professors from Erewhon (as in the work of Butler), members indulge in a cabalistic spectacle of academic parodies, constructing a complicated but meaningless bureaucracy of regents and satraps, who lampoon the institutional arbitrariness of scholastic categories, imitating what Swift calls the "universal artist," the kind of person who might breed sheep without wool so as to advance "speculative learning" (1960, 147). As Taylor remarks: "the *College of 'Pataphysics* promotes 'pataphysics in this world and in all others" (Taylor 1960, 151).

The College of 'Pataphysics strives to substantiate the imaginary philosophy that Butler in turn has hypothesized for his own College of Unreason—a philosophy that Butler calls "hypothetics" (the nowhere science of Erewhon). Such a *Philosophie des Als Ob* imagines a set of impossible exigencies, each of which requires the sophistry of a possible solution: "[to] require the youths to give intelligent answers to the questions that arise therefrom, is reckoned the fittest conceivable way of preparing them for the actual conduct of their affairs" (Butler [1872] 1970, 185–86). To teach only the reality of the *as is* without thought for the *as if* is to invite the myopia of a fixed logic: after all, an extreme science always risks the peril of its own folly. No errors are so egregious that reason cannot find a wily means to defend, at all cost, their impugned prestige.

The College of 'Pataphysics subscribes implicitly to such an Erewhonian hypothesis: the idea that, if unreason cannot exist without its opposite, then surely an increase in the former must result in an increase in the latter (hence, the need to advocate what is specious in order to expedite what is rational) (Butler [1872] 1970, 187).[2] The "double currency" of such a surrational perspective sustains a deconstructive undecidability between syllogism and sophistry (insofar as logic is used to prove that logic itself cannot be used to prove): "[t]he Professors of Unreason deny that they undervalue reason: none can be more convinced than they are, that if the double currency cannot be rigorously deduced . . . , the double currency [must] cease forthwith" (108). The *meta* of physics must be invalid if it cannot reveal to itself the *pata* of its own madness.

The College of 'Pataphysics offers no degree for such a lesson but simply grants pupils the permission to indulge in the kind of epistemological experimentation seen, for example, in the abstract workshop of Oulipo (where sober whimsy reconciles work and play in order to reassert the rigorous pleasure of cerebral exercise). For Queneau, such disciplined daydreaming requires a radical science of willful naïveté: "[w]e forge ahead without undue refinement" since "[w]e try to prove motion by walking" ([1950] 1986a, 51). Such a nomadic science privileges the amateurism of tinkering engineers, who proceed by trial and error, case by case, following rather than directing a course of action: not refinement, but engagement. Such rigorous activity is simply a diversion that follows a *clinamen* in the traject of thought.

The Bureau of Surrealism

The College of 'Pataphysics has in turn inspired a conceptual laboratory that does not simply repeat the ironies of either Lagado or Erewhon; instead, the surrationalism of *l'ouvroir de littérature potentielle* serves to oppose the irrationalism of *le bureau de récherches surréalistes*. While Artaud might argue that such a bureau must reinterpret inspiration, according to "an order that is impossible to elucidate by the methods of ordinary reason" ([1925] 1976, 105), the project of such a bureau does, nevertheless, differ from the project of Oulipo. While Artaud insists that Surrealism must follow no formula (106), Lionnais insists that Oulipianism must sample every formula: "the goal of potential literature is to furnish future writers with new techniques which can dismiss inspiration from their affectivity" (Lescure [1973] 1986, 38).

While the bureau provides a facility where the public might record its dreams (for the sake of a future study), Oulipo provides a workshop where a quorum might invent new charts (for the sake of a future dream). Just as Futurism swerves away from the influence of Symbolism, so also does Oulipianism swerve away from the influence of Surrealism—even though all four aesthetics oppose the metaphysics of reason itself. Both the Surrealists and the Oulipians may subscribe to a belief in the automatism of writing; however, the Oulipians reject the belief that freedom is born from the haphazard rejection of a structured constraint, arguing that the surreal concept of blind chance mistakenly buttresses the idea that radical thought can be based upon systematic ignorance. For Oulipo, no rule can be undermined by pretending that the rule does not exist.

Oulipo agrees with the surreal premise that concepts of the true can no longer provide a standard for the paradigm of the real; however, Oulipo argues that to prove this point by completely abandoning a rational axiology is to commit a surreal mistake. Roubaud suggests that, to avoid this error, Oulipo proposes to envision a kind of "mathematical surrealism" ([1981] 1986, 80), in which *mathema* coincides perfectly with *poiesis* (insofar as both domains refer to the surrealist virtuality of an *as if*—the *Traumwelt* of our own suspended disbelief). Even a calculus textbook can speculate about a set of alternate realities, each with its own rational modality (be it a tesseract, a null-space, etc.). For Oulipo, the speculations of such mathematics are no less surreal than the radical poetics of a bureaucratized oneirocriticism.

Oulipo interprets such revisions of exception as a form of paradoxical temporality that, like Futurism, reverses causality through a simulacral precession. Influence becomes an act of "plagiarism by anticipation" ([1973] 1986, 31) in which, by some swerve, a past style merely replicates what a future style has already originated. What Lionnais calls "anoulipism" (the analysis of a past constraint) may inspire what Lionnais calls "synthoulipism" (the synthesis of a future potential)—but this subsequent potential in turn revises its precedent constraint through a kind of 'pataphysical retroversion. Such a reversal is not surreal in its nostalgia so much as oneiric in its prognosis. As Lionnais suggests, "[i]t is possible to compose texts that have . . . surrealist . . . qualities without having qualities of potential" (Lescure [1973] 1986, 38).[3]

Mathematics and 'Pataphysics

Inspired by the College of 'Pataphysics, Oulipo attempts to propose a 'pataphysical counterpoint to the rational axiology of mathematics. Some members of the College, such as Queneau and Arnaud (who are also members of Oulipo) have traced the spirals of their own cognitive *gidouille,* deriving the reductio ad absurdum of an impossible hypothesis: just as Queneau studies the aerodynamics of equations (1950, 21), so also does Arnaud explain the mathematics of umbrellas (1955, 48). What the College has studied on behalf of the *clinamen* has in turn influenced the studies of Oulipo itself (particularly the literary research of its mathematical professionals: Lionnais, Roubaud, Braffort, et al.—all of whom pursue research inspired less by the rectilinear *Compars* of Euclid and more by the curvilinear *Dispars* of Riemann).

Oulipo merely follows, then extends, the *clinamen* already present in the numerical sophistry of Jarry, who attributes the origin of science to an ancient geometry, the "[']Pataphysics of Sophrotatos" ([1911] 1965, 251), from which a Pythagorean philosopher might derive the formula for the *syzygia:* (±). When Faustroll uses the algebra of such a formula in order to calculate that God is equal to the tangent between nihility and infinity (Jarry [1911] 1965, 256), Jarry parodies the metaphysical scholasticism of Pascal by suggesting that belief in the coherence of such logic is no less absurd than belief in the existence of a deity. Such a weird proof only provides an allegory for the argument that science itself coincides with the chiasm between nihility and infinity, since the limit of its error (±)—as a measurement of uncertainty—must likewise remain absolute.

Oulipo also follows, then extends, the *clinamen* already present in the numerical sophistry of Marinetti, who attributes the future of science to an updated calculus, in which "[t]he mathematical signs + - × serve to achieve marvelous syntheses" ([1914] 1991, 111). When Marinetti imagines a poetry of lyrical numbers, he argues that, "[w]ith the mathematical *x,* the doubting suspension suddenly spreads itself over the entire agglomeration of words-in-freedom," thereby eliminating any question which localizes its doubt upon only one point of awareness (110); instead, every potentiality is considered in its simultaneity, be it plus or minus (±).[4] Such equations suggest that, "by (addressing themselves phonically and optically to the numerical sensibility)" (110), 'pataphysicians might reveal the potential for a chiasm between *mathema* and *poiesis.*

Roubaud argues that, for Oulipo, to compose poetry is to undertake a mathetic analysis of language itself (so that eventually every poem might provide a given proof for some literary formula): "[w]riting under . . . constraint is . . . equivalent [to] the drafting of a mathematical text, which may be formalized according to the axiomatic method" ([1981] 1986, 89). Like Buchanan, who proposes treating metaphor mathematically and mathesis metaphorically (1929, 13) in order to explore their reciprocal influences, Oulipo endeavors to demonstrate that only through the hybridity of such 'pataphysical dilettantism can science hope to express the novelty of anomaly.[5] Just as advances in the nomic tradition of *mathema* depend upon a ludic sedition against the numerary, so also do advances in the nomic tradition of *poiesis* depend upon a ludic sedition against the literary.

Queneau, for example, willfully misreads the premises of Hilbert (who speculates that for the axioms of Euclid, such terms as "point," "curve," or "plane" can go by any name without affecting the structural legitimacy of the axiom itself) ([1976] 1995, 4); hence, Queneau translates these axioms by replacing the three geometric terms with three grammatical terms (morpheme, phraseme, ideomeme) so that the standard definition of a straight line (as an infinite sequence of points) becomes the humorous definition of a literary line: "[e]very sentence contains an infinity of words"—some are perceived; most are imaginary (13). Such an intertextual substitution of *poiesis* for *mathema* produces an aphorism about the potentialities of intertextuality itself—the idea that "[b]etween two words of a sentence there exists an infinity of other words" (13).

Queneau dramatizes such 'pataphysical potentiality by demonstrating his own "parallel postulate," in which the *poiesis* of any genre might be transposed into the *mathema* of some axiom. Every conic curve provides a metaphor for the *clinamen* of a given trope: the elliptical function of abbreviation, the paraboloid function of disquisition, and the hyperbolic function of exaggeration (Queneau [1976] 1995, 15). Like an equation, each of the axiomatic sentences is itself a constraint for a set of variables (be they geometrical or grammatical). The permuting of these variables generates a paradoxical formulation, whose Gödelian reasoning imposes a constraint upon the potentials of constraint itself: that is, "[a]xioms are not governed by axioms" (7). The rule is that, for every rule whose structure is reflexive (including this rule), the swerve of an exception must intervene.

The Exception of Constraint

Oulipo derives its own exceptional formalities from the *mathema* of "combinatorics"—a discipline that studies what Berge calls "configurations": "[a] *configuration* arises every time objects are distributed according to . . . constraints" ([1968] 1971, 1).[6] Such a science pertains to the optimization of arrangements within determined parameters. What applies, for example, to the nomic study of numerals in matrices might also be applied to the ludic study of Latinate squares and Scrabble puzzles.[7] The fixed canon of literary research has often ignored the nomadic anomaly of such combinatorics on the assumption that to subscribe to constraint is to indulge in a frivolous aesthetic even though the formality of such constraint (as seen, for example, in the acrostic, in the lipogram, and in the rhopalic) can potentially afford the study of poetics with the rigor of a science.

Perec complains that "formal mannerisms . . . are relegated to the registers of asylums" wherein "[c]onstraints are treated . . . as aberrations" ([1973] 1986, 98), even though the values of such a radical poetics depend not upon the significance of its themes but upon the extravagance of its schema. Like Futurism, which rejects passéism, Oulipo argues that a poetry of the future must absorb, not avoid, what is paradoxical and paralogical in the science of the present, since to reject the sedition of the new is simply to adopt the tradition of the old, maintaining unconscious constraints without an appraisal of constraint itself. The distinction between *poiesis* and *mathema* is a constraint that has outlived its potential, and thus the 'pataphysician must disrupt this constraint by adopting, as a new constraint, *mathema* itself.

Bénabou suggests that to appeal to an aesthetics of constraint is to reveal the hidden agenda, the secret power, in the pragmatics of all constraint: "to the extent that constraint goes beyond rules which seem natural only to those people who have barely questioned language, it forces the system out of its routine functioning, thereby compelling it to reveal its hidden resources" ([1983] 1986, 41). As Queneau suggests, "inspiration which consists in blind obedience to every impulse is in reality a sort of slavery" because "the poet who writes that which comes into his head . . . is the slave of other rules of which he is ignorant" (Bénabou [1983] 1986, 41). To explore the rule is to be emancipated from it by becoming the master of *its potential for surprise,* whereas to ignore the rule is to be imprisoned in it by becoming the slave to *the reprise of its intention.*

Roubaud argues that, to realize the potentiality of such a radical poetics, "a constraint [is] envisaged only on the condition that this text contain all the *possibilities* of the constraint" ([1981] 1986, 95)—which is to say that the constraint must comprehensively evoke the entire domain of its own *as if,* producing not an exemplary singularity to be repeated but an imaginary multiparity to be explored. Such a literary manifold does not produce a variation upon its own significant themes so much as produce an extravagant scheme of variation. What is potential generates a new process rather than an old product. The exception to a rule implies not a freedom from but the outcome of such an exhaustive constraint. The exception explicates the rule, testing its limits, defying its fields, forsaking the nomic work of one paradigm for the ludic risk of another paralogy.

Roubaud argues that the potential of such a constraint can avoid the imperialism of its own repetition if the constraint, when proposed, produces only one textual example: "there even exists a tendency, which might be qualified as *ultra,* for which *every* text deduced from a constraint must be classed in the 'applied' domain, the only admissible text, for the Oulipian . . . being the text that formulates the constraint and, in so doing, exhausts it" ([1981] 1986, 91). While the constraints of Oulipo can tend toward multiple examples only by ceasing to perform the intentions of Oulipo, such a *constraint upon constraint* omits the necessity for deduction in the method itself. Even though a constraint must provide only a virtual theorem about a hypothetical textuality, such a theorem must "prove" itself through at least one imagined solution.

Roubaud argues that, in effect, a text written according to a constraint must speak of this constraint (1981, 90), if only because this constraint upon constraint dramatizes the reflexive tautology of *mathema* itself (hence, a writer like Perec might compose a lipogram that refers to itself *as a lipogram,* repressing the letter E while mentioning the absent E: "I [would] start giving my plotting a symbolic turn, so that . . . it would point up, without blatantly divulging, that Law that was its inspiration, that Law from which it would draw . . . a rich, fruitful narration" ([1969] 1994, 282). Such a strict but absurd law about law nevertheless dramatizes a perverse allegory about 'pataphysics itself (as if to suggest that reality is merely a system of arbitrary constraint, whose rules have created a science that can in turn discuss such rules).

Constraint provides an allegory for the phenomenal recurrence of a numerical structure so that, like Fibonacci sequences (which subtend the natural anatomy of nautili and flowers), such acts of *poietic mathema* evoke 'pataphysical speculations about the ludic basis of reality itself (implying that physics is merely the poetic effect of a vast game that reality must play—a game in which the rules themselves are at stake). As Roubaud argues, "something 'additional to' their production intervenes, different from the secrets of their enumeration: the search for a new multiplicity of limits (or of non-limits . . .), each the founder of a remarkable . . . proposition, a number no longer golden, but made of some other precious element, [the] 'rare earth' of esthetics" ([1981] 1986, 96)—the ironic verity of beauty.

The Exception of Potential

Greimas quotes de Tracy in order to argue that no narrative game lacks imperative rules: "[o]ne should beware of believing [that] the inventive mind operates according to chance" ([1968] 1987, 48). Oulipo agrees with Greimas, insofar as it refuses to equate chance with a freedom from some dictum. Bens, however, wonders in what way "one [can] reconcile such rigor with . . . the incertitude . . . that [must] necessarily accompany potentiality" ([1981] 1986, 70), and he suggests that Oulipo does so by evoking the *syzygia* as a trope for the ambivalent relativity between the *alea* and the *fata*. Oulipo explores the poetic impact of any aleatoric form that arises paradoxically from an axiomatic rule (for example, the random series of digits in the set π or the random series of primes in the set N—arbitrary sequences that reveal a *complicity* between complexity and simplicity).

Queneau cites such mathetic examples of chance in order to swerve away from his Surrealist compatriots (who reject him for his belief that chance does not necessarily synchronize with extreme freedom); instead, chance arises not from the absence of a conscious rule but from the presence of an ineffable rule (Bénabou [1983] 1986, 41). While the Surrealists must insist that the anagrammatic coincidences of *automatic scription* do exemplify the random excess of irrational liberation, Baudrillard has gone so far as to aver that this kind of excess is not so arbitrary as it is mandatory: it is a necessity exceeding the rule which joins the signifier and the signified (a rule which is itself supremely arbitrary) ([1983] 1990a, 151). What is surreal about a rule is not its disappearance, but its reflexiveness: its ability to recognize itself as an exception.

Baudrillard suggests that, for science there exist two hypotheses about chance itself, the first metaphysical (suggesting that all things are disconnected and divergent, and only by chance do they meet each other) and the second 'pataphysical (suggesting that all things are connected and convergent, and only by chance do they miss each other) ([1983] 1990a, 145). While quantum physics has corrected the implicit error within deterministic causality, substituting *alea* for *fata,* such a science has nevertheless disclosed an even more implicit order behind indeterminate causality—a synchronistic order that is coincidental and conspiratory: "[c]hance . . . correspond[s] not to a temporary incapacity of science to explain everything . . . but to the passing from a state of causal determination to another order, radically different, also of non-chance" (145).[8]

Baudrillard suggests that, for science, "[c]hance itself is a special effect; it assumes in imagination the perfection of the accident" ([1983] 1990a, 149)—the kind of accident that characterizes the fatal order of all *poiesis* (particularly in the case of Oulipo): "[w]riting[. . . ,] [w]hether poetry or theory, [is] nothing but the projection of an arbitrary code . . . (an invention of the rules of a game) where things come to be taken in their fatal development" (154). The game presents an arbitrary ensemble of constraints, of necessities, whose outcome remains uncertain. The science of 'pataphysics suggests that the real is a ludic event, whose mandatory fate results from an aleatoric rule that produces not a *reprise of* its code so much as a *surprise from* its code. The *alea* is the *aporia* of the *fata,* revealing the paradox of a so-called random order.

Oulipo suggests that the potentials of constraint coincide with the *poiesis* of a ludic state, whose *mathema* constitutes a playful way to study all that is playful (doing so in a manner different from the kind of statistical rationalism, which codifies play according to a formal matrix of mini-max options and zero-sum tactics). Baudrillard observes that, although what is ludic does not regard the rule of its constraints as a mandatory universal, what is ludic does nevertheless assume that the *as if* of such constraints can free us from the necessities of the *as is:* "by choosing the rule one is delivered from the law"—from its metaphysical prerequisite, that is, belief in the verity of its system (1990b, 133). The truth of the ludic abides by no belief; instead, such truth is *entertained* as one of many hypothetical alternatives. It is merely a "potentiality."

Oulipo proposes the *as if* of such a constraint in order to swerve away from it through the potential of a mandatory exception. Perec explains that, "when a system of constraints is established, there must also be anticonstraint within it" (Motte 1986, 276). Life itself must always include cases of "falsity" and "absence" in the structure of its *mode d'emploi*, either altering or deleting an event so that there remains at least one anomalous component to the puzzle (Perec [1978] 1987, 497). For Perec, a constraint must systematically evoke its own disintegration in a manner that calls to mind the paradox of the Persian flaw (insofar as it perfects what it disrupts): "[t]he system of constraints . . . must not be rigid, there must be some play in it, it must, as they say, 'creak' a bit; it must not be completely coherent; there must be a *clinamen*" (Motte 1986, 276).[9]

Oulipo suggests that the potential of such a *clinamen* evokes a 'pataphysical multiplicity. Bens, for example, observes that, "[s]ince reality never reveals more than a part of its totality, it thereby justifies a thousand interpretations, significations . . . , all equally probable" ([1981] 1986, 72). Just as Bens might argue that "*potentiality,* more than a technique of composition, is a certain way of conceiving the literary" (72), so also does Lescure argue that "every literary text is literary because of an indefinite quantity of potential meanings" ([1973] 1986, 37). What is *potentiality* for the French Oulipians is thus tantamount to *literariness* for the Russian Formalists, insofar as both concepts theorize the *poiesis* of novelty in terms of an *as if,* in which to be literary is to pose imaginary solutions to problematic formalities.[10]

The Anagram of 'Pataphysics

Oulipo regards *poiesis* as a form of *ars combinatoria,* in which the alphabet provides a fixed array of Lucretian particles in a state of disciplined permutation. Bénabou remarks that, since all the different modes of *mathema* (addition, division, etc.) can be applied to all the different strata of *poiesis* (morpheme, phraseme, etc.), a text is just a set of atomistic variables that evolve within a set of axiomatic constants ([1983] 1986, 44–45). Bénabou repeats the premise of Hjelmslev, who argues that, if language is merely a formulaic way of selecting terms and arranging them in a formulaic way, then "an exhaustive calculus of the possible combinations" can be "described by means of a limited number of premisses" ([1943] 1969, 9). This mathetic analysis of language presumes that language has a machinic function: that it is one of many cellular automata.

Greimas, moreover, goes further than anyone in describing such a poietic *mathema,* since his own genre of Structuralism invokes the abstract model of symbolic logic in order to derive the formula for literature itself. Narrative structure can be reduced to an imperial calculus, in which the given units are arranged within magical squares, according to a formal ensemble of Boolean axioms: conjunction, disjunction, nonconjunction, nondisjunction. Meaning arises from "the interaction of semiotic constraints" (Greimas [1968] 1987, 48) within a grammar of reciprocal relativity. Poetic genres simply diagram the transition of "actants" from position to position in this set of quadratic relations. Like the Oulipians, the Structuralists argue that poetic genius can be explained according to a rule.

Mathews has even written poetry according to an algorithm that arranges words within a formal matrix of combinatorial possibilities ([1981] 1986, 126).[11] Such a mathetic analysis of grammatical permutation suggests that even aesthetic constraints might themselves be arranged within a matrix of genres so that just as Mendeleyev can propose a periodic table of chemical elements, so also can Queneau propose a periodic table of poetical elements, both indices acting as atomic diagrams by which to classify the results of poetic programs (Bénabou [1983] 1986, 46). Just as Mendeleyev reveals the relative positions for possible elements (as yet unfound), so also does Queneau reveal the relative positions for potential poetries (as yet untried). Such analysis offers a topography of virtuality, revealing domains of anomaly for futuristic innovation.

Oulipo may appear to repeat the theories of Structuralism, but (as Roubaud observes), "[s]tructure, in its . . . Oulipian sense, has only a minimal relation to 'Structuralism' " ([1981] 1986, 93). Oulipo draws a subtle but urgent distinction between the *Structura* of Greimas and the *Structure* of Queneau: the former describing a static diagram for the general case of a text, the latter inscribing a rhetic program for the special case of a text. *Structura*, for Greimas, corresponds to the predictable reprise of the *Compars*, providing a hermeneutic formula for extracting *constants* from anagrammatic variables: it is a *model product* to be emulated—whereas *Structure*, for Roubaud, corresponds to the unpredictable surprise of the *Dispars*, providing a speculative formula for injecting *variants* into anagrammatic variables: it is a *modal process* to be explored.

Saussure suggests that, for the *Structura* of linguistics, even the radical *poiesis* of the anagram preserves some sort of formula for a constant (usually a deified keyword, whose phonemes are repeated over and over again throughout the poem in order to reconstitute a covert origin of meaning) (Starobinski [1971] 1979, 18). Baudrillard, however, suggests that, for the *Structure* of 'pataphysics, "[t]he symbolic act never consists in the reconstitution of the name of God after a detour . . . within the poem ([1976] 1993a, 199)—instead, the formula of the anagram destroys the keyword, dissecting it, dispersing it, in order to obliterate the remains of any meaning.[12] Whereas the metaphysical atomism of *Structura* reduces words to absolute units that *support signification,* the 'pataphysical atomism of *Structure* reduces words to dissolute units that *subvert signification.*

Baudrillard writes that "[a]ll these formulas converge on the idea of a 'Brownian' stage of language, an emulsional stage of the signifier, homologous to the molecular stage of physical matter, that liberates 'harmonies' of meaning just as fission or fusion liberates new molecular affinities" ([1976] 1993a, 218). When Perec, for example, writes a heterogram, in which each line of a grid contains a different sequence of the ten most common letters (AEILNORSTU) plus one other, he does not simply encipher messages within a tabula that makes sense when read left to right, line by line; instead, he explores the combinatorics of an unanticipated configuration (1985, [7]). Just as the *as if* of a mathematic concept often coincides uncannily with the *as is* of its phenomenal reality, so also does the anagram contrive an unexpected (rather than encipher an antecedent) meaning.

Perec can thus transform a sequence such as ACEILNORSTU into a "factory of exchange" (*l'usine à troc*) which turns howls (*usé cri tonal*) into tools (*outils à soc*), according to a closed system—a matrix of undecennary orderliness: "you have the casket: here, nude, art dares it" (*tu as l'écrin: ci, nu, art l'ose*) (1985, [28]). Rather than encode a cryptic keyword (whose repeated presence might dramatize the "ulcerations" of such a formidable constraint), these anagrams disperse the atomistic particles of such a keyword through a kind of literal seepage (the "ulcerations" evoking, then erasing, the pain of the rule). The anagram does not recycle so much as atomize its meaning, dissecting it, dispersing it, until the keyword vanishes (just as every meaningful phenomenon vanishes through the permuted excesses of its own atomic events).

The Program of 'Pataphysics

Oulipo derives its inspiration for this kind of anagrammatic 'pataphysics from the work of Swift, who conceives "a project for improving speculative knowledge by . . . mechanical operations" ([1726] 1960, 148). What Swift describes with humor in a spirit of moral seriousness, Oulipo practices with humor in a spirit of sober whimsy. What Swift satirizes, Oulipo plagiarizes. Like the projectors at the Grand Academy of Lagado, the professors at *l'ouvroir de littérature potentielle* recombine the *disjecta membra* of a textual history in order to invent an absurd device that can eliminate the necessity for inspiration: "[e]very one knows how laborious the usual method is of attaining to arts and sciences; whereas by . . . contrivance the most ignorant person . . . may write books . . . without the least assistance from genius or study" (Swift [1726] 1960, 148).

Swift imagines a screen across which the spectacle of the *alea* and the *fata* can appear and disappear through the automation of an *ars combinatoria*. The Grand Academy of Lagado creates a framework of wood cubes that swivel on wire axles, their numerous facets covered by square pieces of paper with all the words of the language engraved upon them in all their moods and cases, but without any order, so that anyone turning the handles on the edge of the frame might alter the old sequence of recorded thinking and thus evoke a new sentence.[13] What Swift berates metaphysically as a reckless device, Oulipo equates 'pataphysically with a bachelor engine— the *as if* of a literary computer. Like the Futurists, the Oulipians equate *poiesis* itself with a machinic paralogy (whose potential involves an intended accident—the swerve of anagrammatic coincidences).

Oulipo imagines that such a computer can express the potential of a constraint too laborious to be otherwise fulfilled (since machines can easily perform the exhaustive task of both selecting words and combining them— in a way that has since come to define the mesostics of Cage or the aleatories of Mac Low); however, such acts of prosthetic automation do not simply assist in the *process* of writing so much as replace the *concept* of writing itself. Thomas observes that the prefaces to poems by Oulipo do not serve as authorial statements about semantic intention; instead, they comprise a *mode d'emploi,* not unlike a README.DOC that precedes a computer program (1981, 18). A text is no longer simply a *message* produced by, and for, a person, so much as it is a *program* produced by, and for, a device—an algorithm designed to make its reader become a writer.

Oulipo imagines that such a cybernetic literature of anagrammatic permutations might realize the dream of Borges and create a garden of forking paths—an interactive experience of rhizomatic potentials, in which the machine expects the reader to behave like a writer who must deflect the course of the narrative through an ensemble of crucial options—the *as if* of multiple *if thens.* What Queneau calls a "tree literature" ([1973] 1986b, 156) and what Fournel calls a "theater tree" ([1973] 1986, 159) have come to represent some of the first texts to discuss the potential for interactive innovations (particularly hypertexts). Such cases of cybernetic literature begin to dramatize a philosophy of 'pataphysical perspectivism, insofar as they attempt to imagine a multitude of divergent realities created simultaneously from the same text.

Queneau in *Cent Mille Milliards de poèmes* perhaps offers the first such case study in his attempt to produce a book that is not so much a volume for storing poetry as a machine for creating poetry: ten sonnets are written on ten pages with cut lines so that a line from any sonnet can be supplanted by its cognate from any of the other sonnets (while still preserving all their rules of rhythm and syntax). Since the Cartesian product of ten sonnets with fourteen lines (10^{14}) permits trillions of different cases, a single reader, reading one a second, must survive for more than a thousand millennia in order to read every poem. Such a book remains inscrutable not because of its illegibility but because of its potentiality. Such a book is 'paraphysical, insofar as it deals with the *as if* of what is possible in virtuality but impossible in actuality.

While Queneau apparently thematizes the idea of inexhaustible signification (*ars longa, vita brevis*), his text nevertheless demonstrates that "[a]rt is not long enough even in the shortest of lives" (Oulipo [1973] 1986, 48) since the onerous, if not sublime, burden of all the unexplored potentials must always outweigh the durability of any one text: "[t]he *Cent Mille Milliards de poèmes* [has] rendered this clear to [']pataphysicians" (48). No poem can endure long enough to resist all the new poems that it in turn evokes. It too is merely the intimation of a future text that is likewise unreadable *in its absolute entirety* because it too is no more than a virtual machine for creating the possible: "Poetic licence needs no strain or stress / One tongue will do to keep the verse agog / From cool Parnassus down to wild Loch Ness / Bard I adore your endless monologue" (Oulipo [1961] 1998, 29).

Oulipo regards such a poem as a kind of literary computer, whose power resides in its ability to graph a "map of . . . virtualities" (Oulipo [1973] 1986, 50) — a map that alludes to the increasing role of industrial machines in all aspects of *poiesis:* "[t]his exploration . . . only begins to suggest the vastness . . . explorable when . . . thanks to computers we can finally . . . begin to reveal the constants of a writer in all sorts of areas" (49–50). Such a poem produces an "effect . . . of mystification" (50), defamiliarizing the romantic mystique of irrationalism by providing a parenthetical example in the present for a hypothetical machine of the future — a machine able to peruse the poetry of humans even as it writes poetry of its own: "being, like Swift, skeptical prophets, we entertain these prospects [']pataphysically" (50).

Mathetic Machines

Calvino argues that "the aid of a computer, far from *replacing* the creative act of the artist, permits the latter rather to liberate himself from the slavery of a combinatory search, allowing him also the best chance of concentrating on this *'clinamen'* which, alone, can make of the text a true work of art" ([1981] 1986a, 152). Computerized experiments with poetry so far resemble Surrealism because they mimic aleatory impulses (chance forms, random styles, broken logic); however, the creativity of machinery might be better served by the mannerism of its formal rigor: "[t]he true literature machine [is] one that itself feels the need to produce disorder, as a reaction against its preceding production of order: a machine that [can] produce avant-garde work to free its circuits when they are choked by too long a production of classicism" (Calvino [1967] 1986b, 13).

Calvino suggests that, because cybernetics has begun to develop machines capable of autodidactics and autopoetics, "nothing prevents us from foreseeing a literature machine that at a certain point feels unsatisfied with its own traditionalism and starts to propose new ways of writing, turning its own codes completely upside down" ([1967] 1986b, 13). Such a machine might analyze the material relations between poetics and history by correlating its own stylistic variation to the stock index: "[t]hat indeed will be the literature that corresponds perfectly to a theoretical hypothesis: it will, at last, be *the* literature" (13).[14] While the Surrealists argue that, because inspiration is instinctive, it is inexplicable, the Oulipians argue that what is most automatistic in the instinct of writing must also therefore be most *programmable*.

Oulipo suggests that "[t]he Word is . . . ontogenetically [']pataphysical" ([1973] 1986, 48), insofar as language does not depict the world of the *as is* so much as create the world of the *as if:* "[t]he time of the *created creations . . .* should cede to the era of *creating creations*" (48) — not artifacts but catalysts: not *objets d'art* but *modes d'emploi*. Poetry is no longer the *effect of* inspiration so much as it is the *cause for* inspiration: "[t]he whole world of literature ought to become the object of numerous . . . prostheses" ([1973] 1986, 31), be they linguistic or cybernetic.[15] For Oulipo, inspiration is ultimately not irrational so much as it is surrational. Its creativity results from the *fata* of a simple law that applies itself to itself to form the *alea* of a complex art. The swerve of a *clinamen* arises from the rigor of such influence.

Oulipo implies that each text ought to become no more than a tool to be deployed upon itself by yet another text in order to produce "a Topology of Commonplaces, in which one . . . succeed[s] in abstracting commonplaces from the structures of commonplaces—and then a 'squared' topology of these places . . . until one attains, in a rigorous analysis of this *regressus* itself, the absolute" ([1973] 1986, 50). Oulipo, however, introduces a *clinamen* into the metaphysics of such an absolute. The repetition of a past constraint (the *regressus*) swerves into the intimation of a future potential (the *digressus*). The machinic accident of such a swerve threatens the existential originality of creativity by reminding the poet about the potential iterability of creativity itself. The science of 'pataphysics must eventually evoke even its own 'pataphysical retroversion.

Palaeontology reigns, it would seem over a kind of criminal unconscious of the species, since this race for fossils, this forced exploration bears a strange resemblance to the exploring of the fossils of the unconscious. Each has about it the same ressentiment as to our origins.

—Baudrillard [1992] 1994a, 72

In the world of 'Pataphysics, Canada is Nowhere.

—Wershler-Henry 1994, 66

5. Canadian "Pataphysics

A 'Pataphysics of Mnemonic Exception

The Nowhere Science

Canadian Jarryites present the third case for the surrationalism of the 'pataphysical, revising the structure of exception in order to oppose the irrationalism of Canadian Nationalists. The Canadian Jarryites respond to the avant-garde pseudoscience of Jarry by inflecting the mnemonic intensities of paleological forms, arguing that exception results from the corruption of memories. The Canadian Jarryites have included such poets as McCaffery, Nichol, and Dewdney, all of whom have parodied the environmental mythopoiesis of such critics as Frye, Atwood, and Kroetsch (for whom literature is merely the side effect of a geography—the surreal terrain of a collective unconscious). Like Futurism and Oulipism, Canadian "Pataphysics opposes such mysticism, treating literature not as a mythopoeic but as a cyborganic phenomenon.

Canadian "Pataphysics reveals that any attempt by Canada to define a coherent identity for its own state in response to the dominant identity of another state (be it European or American) simply reifies the metaphysics of the state itself (its nationalism, its imperialism). Canadian "Pataphysics resorts to Jarry in order to parody the metaphysics of both Canadian autonomy and European hegemony—but by doing so, such "Pataphysics ironically reifies the European hegemony of 'pataphysics itself. Wershler-Henry observes that for the cartography of 'pataphysics, "Canada is Empty"

(1994, 66), *sous rature,* since the map for the College of 'Pataphysics does not include such a country in its sphere of influence—even though the map appears, ironically enough, in an issue of the *Dossiers* that discusses the very 'pataphysics of the arctic (Fassio 1961, 30–31).

Wershler-Henry suggests that, despite the intent of Jarry to address the paralogy of all such eccentricity, the legacy of Jarry may have served only to install the ubiquity of his own centrality. Wershler-Henry suggests that, despite the paradox of this oversight, Canadian Jarryites have done little to unveil their obscured presence so that, for Canada, "[t]he "pataphysical field remains perpetually open, [a] 'smooth space' that baffles State attempts at philosophical containment" (1994, 67). Canadian "Pataphysics marks its difference from its imperial cousin ('Pataphysics) through a swerve (*clinamen*) (67), resorting to European 'pataphysics in order to parody European 'pataphysics, granting Canada its own autonomy from the question of autonomy itself by portraying these paradoxical endeavors as an imagined solution to mnemonic problems.

Canadian Jarryites make a spectacle of thematic banality by presenting their own brand of archaeological misinformation, reducing such a mnemonic paradigm to a set of 'pataphysical expenditures. Rather than indulge in mythomania, Jarryites resort to the tropes of the *anomalos,* the *syzygia,* and the *clinamen* in order to create their own forms of satirical criticism (be it the probable systems of Nichol, the perseus projects of McCaffery, or the natural histories of Dewdney). This kind of nomadic science does not attempt to portray the essence of its own culture; instead, such criticism strives to present the play of wonder over wisdom, evoking what Dewdney might call "a universe where what we consider uncanny . . . occurs almost ten times as frequently" (1982, 30)—a universe that in the end turns out to be none other than our own.

Quotidian Quotation

McCaffery and Nichol write that "Canadian "Pataphysics quite clearly is a literature that, as yet, has no archive," and "[i]ts absence of inscription superbly parallels its absence of thought" (Toronto Research Group [hereafter TRG] 1992, 303). Wershler-Henry observes that Canadian "Pataphysics eludes definition because "many Canadian "Pataphysicists share the affinity of the European and American colleagues for dissimulation" (1994, 68), with individuals coexisting under various pseudonyms amid various collectives, be they actual or unreal: for example, the Toronto Research Group, the Institute of Linguistic Ontogenetics, and the "Pataphysical Hardware Company. Canadian "Pataphysics does indeed mimic the 'pataphysics of such European institutes as *le collège de 'pataphysique* or *l'ouvroir de littérature potentielle;* however, such a science marks its difference from European 'pataphysics through a change in diacritical orthography.

Canadian "Pataphysics adds another vestigial apostrophe to its name in order to mark not only the excess silence *imposed upon* Canadians by a European avant-garde but also the ironic speech *proposed by* Canadians against a European avant-garde. McCaffery and Nichol suggest that Canadian "Pataphysics moves from elision (') to quotation (") through a superinducement on elision — "the doubling of the elide, a doubled inversion and [an] inverted doubling" (TRG 1992, 301). A parody of parody itself, such 'pataphysics performs a *clinamen* upon its own history, simulating it (through quotation) while disrupting it (through deviation). The unknown origins of 'pataphysics are explained by the unknown science of 'pataphysics: "the quotation . . . of the given that we do not understand but with emendations that serve to constitute our explanation" (301–2).

Canadian "Pataphysics suggests that its dual but open quote signifies a "portmanteau confluence" (TRG 1992, 301) of the *meta* (beyond) and the *para* (beside), situating itself within a place both external and supernal — a place that, like Canada, is defined paradoxically by its placelessness: the interzone of Ethernity. The open quote for such a science marks the openness of a site that must cite its own openness.[1] Its space does not tell the whole truth because it never has the last word. To quote truth in such a space is to engage in an endless process of eruptive aperture, "the [s]cience of the never-ending, never-commencing discourse" (302) — a science without a fixed ground for generalization, only a fluid field for specialization: "Our whole can only be our part. This is the stated openness of our quotation" (303).

Canadian "Pataphysics quotes European 'Pataphysics in order to parody the mythic desire in Canada for an autonomous, if not indigenous, archetype of mnemonic identity, be it the theme of pastoralism, as in the case of Frye (1971, 241) or the theme of survivalism, as in the case of Atwood (1972, 32). Such criticism seeks to establish a mnemonic paradigm of originality through an act that Kroetsch might call "archaeology" (1989, 2) — a term allegedly borrowed from Foucault but misunderstood by Kroetsch, who attributes to it a hermeneutic connotation that Foucault is careful to avoid. As Davey suggests, this kind of mnemonic thematism is a reductive endeavor, often characterized by simplistic misprision (1983, 3). At best, such criticism is nothing more than a poor case of unconscious 'pataphysics, largely unaware of its own philosophic absurdities.

Irrational Institutes

Canadian Jarryites parody the academic banality of such critics by proposing a philosophic alternative to be studied by irrational institutes: the Toronto Research Group, the Institute for Linguistic Ontogenetics, and the "Pataphysical Hardware Company—virtual cartels that act as marginal cognates for the academies of Laputa or Erewhon.[2] Like *le collège de 'pataphysique* or *l'ouvroir de littérature potentielle,* such phantasmatic institutions comprise a Canadian set of 'pataphysical laboratories, all of which explore the poetics of anomaly, on the assumption that literary research must be more experimental than instrumental: "all research is symbiotic & cannot exist separate from writing," and "where action eliminates the need for writing[,] research can function to discover new uses for potentially outdated forms" (TRG 1992, 23).

Imaginary academies such as these all imply that the mythic desire for cultural essences can only reinforce the metaphysical theorization of an imperial paradigm. Unlike research, theories do not necessarily involve an ad hoc exploration of writing *during* the process of writing but involve a de facto exploitation of writing *after* the process of writing. All theories face their object with autocratic stances and imperative tactics. All theories in effect subordinate thought to the nomic instrumentalism of a royal science, whereas research coordinates thought through the ludic experimentalism of a nomad science. For the research of such imaginary academies, language itself represents a cyborganic phenomenon, in which every text becomes a poetic device, a novel brand of "book-machine," whose virologic mechanism uses us more than we use it.[3]

The Toronto Research Group, for example, rejects univocal theories in favor of dialogic research, replacing the scientific individual with the collective endeavor of "a synthetic subject (based on a *We-full,* not an *I-less* paradigm)" (TRG 1992, 10–11). Rather than embrace the royal imperialism of an objective science, such a think tank studies the nomad radicalism of a sophistic science, arguing that because "all theory is transient & after the fact of writing" (23), the poetic research of a "pataphysician differs from the noetic theories of a metaphysician: "these reports make no pretence to a professorial legitimation" (12); instead, they risk the propriety of reasoning itself through the theoretical eclecticism of "synthetic proposals" (10–11).

Such research provides a ludic alibi for the mnemonic paralogy of a radical science.

The Institute for Linguistic Ontogenetics likewise rejects a royal paradigm in favor of a nomad paralogy, replacing the theories of structural linguistics with the research of *linguistic ontogenetics,* "a tool for prying mankind from . . . set mental attitudes towards language—set attitudes which, for the most part, are based upon linguistic superstition" (Writers 1985, 44). Rather than reprise a fixed array of semic forms, such a think tank invents its own mathetic axiology, one that defines language in terms not of an objective structure but of a "projective wordstruct," whose forms do not depict so much as create reality through a kind of quantum physics, or lingual atomism, which Truhlar describes as "chronospatiodynamic" (1980–81, 102). Such research also provides a ludic alibi for the mnemonic paralogy of a radical science.

The "Pataphysical Hardware Company, moreover, imagines an applied science that might utilize such surrational innovations in order to produce an array of marketable commodities—"[e]verything for your imaginary needs" (Nichol 1993, 115): not blank paper, but "Genuine Brand Blank Verse"; not plaster dust, but "Jarry Brand Plaster de Paris"; not rose seeds, but "Grow Your Own Stein Poem." Such a project does not celebrate a functional technology so much as satirize the linguistic dysfunction of the object itself, its potential to be deployed in any way imaginable, despite the standard function for which it has been normally designed. Such objects parody the fetishes of a capital economy, whose *phynance* encourages conspicuous consumption (among other imaginary solutions) in order to fulfill a panoply of desires that do not exist.

Irrational institutes such as these are as ephemeral as a toy balloon with the word "thought" written upon it. The owner of such "Pataphysical Hardware might dramatize the act of "pataphysics itself by inserting the inflated balloon into a headband, literally producing a comic-strip thought bubble that is in turn destroyed through the use of an accompanying "thought suppressant"—a pin. Such an allegorical destruction of reason characterizes the whimsy of what McCaffery might call a "'pataphysicalized (f)unction" (1980–81, 12)—an exercise in "FUTILITY, which, expressed as F + UTILITY becomes that . . . which is ONE LETTER BEYOND UTILITY" (12). The letter F symbolizes the excess of anomalous exception—"the play of FREEDOM . . . WITHIN FUNCTION" (12): that is, what supplements the "unction" of an otherwise reassuring, but inhibiting, purpose.

Rational Geomancy

Canadian "Pataphysics suggests that the mythomania of thematic thinkers is a kind of unconscious 'pataphysics that takes place in what Wurstwagen calls "the oscillating no-place of speculative geology" (1980–81, 150). Wershler-Henry observes that such paleology represents a "lexical chain that runs through the strata of Canadian "Pataphysics like a vein of precious metal, linking disparate elements in intriguing ways" (1994, 68). "Pataphysics swerves away from the royal science of geology toward the nomad science of geognosy—imagining a rational geomancy that can oppose a national geography: "[w]e mean by Rational Geomancy the acceptance of a multiplicity of means . . . to reorganize those energy patterns we perceive in literature," and "[b]y *energy pattern* we mean that configuration of discharges . . . arising from . . . engagement with a text" (TRG 1992, 153).

Geomancy normally involves an art of divination by interpreting the signs of the earth, its telluric rhythms and tectonic stresses. Such a discipline involves a realignment of topographies. Parts are arranged to produce ley lines of force; cracks are read as fault lines in a form. To read is a seismic act that makes a *schiz,* a shift, in the relation of these parts to each other, either fusing them together or rending them apart. To be a rational geomancer is to apply this model of reading not only to the land (the *as is* of the ontic) but also to a text (the *as if* of the semic): "the geomantic view of literature sees interpretation as any system of alignment" (TRG 1992, 153). A rational geomancer uses 'pataphysics to rechart the fault lines that separate reason from unreason, realigning the nationalist cartography of both a terrain and its culture.

Canadian "Pataphysics suggests that rational geomancy deploys the exception of the *clinamen* in order to read *against the grain:* that is, such geomancy involves a radicalized realignment in the very idea of geomancy itself. Whereas a thematic pedagogue (such as Atwood or Frye) interprets sovereign geography as a metaphysical cipher for a mythic memory (believing such a "myth" to be true), a rational geomancer interprets memory itself as a 'pataphysical cipher for an imaginary landscape (believing the "true" to be a myth). What Truhlar calls "psychopaleontology" refers to this geomantic principle of memory: "the theory that societies . . . unconsciously determine . . . their . . . biological destinies through the procreative force of their languages" (1985, [2]). Such a mnemonic paradigm regards culture as nothing more than a geographic simulacrum.

Wurstwagen, for example, indulges in 'pataphysical archaeology by misreading a Muskokan water tower as a Yucatan sky temple, "as if the architecture [has] framed a discourse in which stone [is] speaking to stone without the clumsy intermediary of the human mind" (1980–81, 148). Wurstwagen misreads the evidence of the structure in order to argue that historians have misread the structure of evidence itself. Canadian history has occulted its potential for the occulting of Canadian history. The very "mythobastardization" (144) that he vilifies in others, he practices himself—but only to imply that all such standardized knowledge is bastardized knowledge. The *clinamen* in the form of his argument parallels the *clinamen* in the form of the ziggurat: "a dominant aesthetic . . . of telluric rhyme . . . and energic *clinamen*" (145).

Wurstwagen argues that the absence of writing on this ancient obelisk stems from a stone taboo, "the strict injuncture that no man shall write upon the stone-that-is-already-written" (1980–81, 149). Unlike any other petroglyphic civilization, this bizarre culture does not *write messages upon* the rock, but *reads messages into* the rock. The archaeologist plots the evolution of an aboriginal settlement from a reading culture (that is agraphic) to a writing culture (that is dyslexic). All writing emerges from this functional illiteracy only as a kind of occluded vagrancy—a "topographic cipher" (153) that acts as a palimpsest, mimicking the writing in the granite while deviating from the writing in the granite. All writing becomes a "vacuscript" (153)—not an absence of writing so much as a writing of absence.

Canadian Jarryites suggest that such a vacuscript coincides with "pataphysics itself, insofar as its imaginary solutions code their own existence into the form of their own nonexistence. Such a fantastic portrait of a Meso-American past in effect provides a satirical allegory for Anglo-Canadian life—a culture that has also practiced its own absurd version of the stone taboo: at first, the culture only reads other books while its own books go unwritten; and then later, the culture writes its own books, which in turn go unread. The "pataphysical taboo of this regional mythology parodies the metaphysical dream of a national narrative. The vacuscript may have no readership—but, as McCaffery suggests, "[w]hen the book is closed, it becomes the SPECULATIVE TEXT imagined and written outside of an actual writing" (1980–81, 12).

Canadian "Pataphysics parodies the exotic status of Canada—the otherness of what Baudrillard might call the *phantasie* of Patagonia: "[t]he disappearance of the Indians, your own disappearance, that of all culture, all landscape, in the bleakness of your mists and ice" ([1990] 1993b, 149). Baudrillard argues that, for such geographic dispersion, "[t]he last word here is that it is better to put an end to a process of creeping disappearance (ours) by means of a live sojourn in a *visible* form of disappearance" — "[t]hat is why 'Patagonia' goes so well with 'Pataphysics,' which is the science of imaginary solutions" (149). Canadian "Pataphysics performs an agonistic spectacle, responding to the disappearance of Patagonia with a hyperbole of its own disappearance, as if "[a]ll translations into action are imaginary solutions" (149).

Like the Futurists and the Oulipians, the Jarryites prefer the ludic speculation of the *as if* to the nomic articulation of the *as is*. They strive to create what McCaffery might call a " 'patatext" (1980–81, 13) — a kind of vacuscript whose reading eludes the instrumentalism of an imperial semantic by putting the notion of play itself *into play*. Such a 'patatextual sensibility characterizes the nomadic studies of Jarryites, who resort to the tropes of the *anomalos,* the *syzygia,* and the *clinamen* in order to create their own forms of satirical criticism (be it the probable systems of Nichol, the perseus projects of McCaffery, or the natural histories of Dewdney). As Dewdney might imply, such criticism reveals that "[t]he poet [is] in the same vanguard of research as physics, molecular chemistry, and pure mathematics" (1980–81, 21).

Probable Systems

Nichol defies the imperial paradigm of paleology in order to propose his own "pataphysical archaeology about the Canadian frontier. Nichol willfully misreads the *mathema* (rather than the *poiesis*) of historiographic interpretation in order to extract an improbable secret from a geological syntax. For Nichol, all of history becomes an imaginary solution to the millenary problems of memory, and despite the ironic title of his "probable systems," such a pathological hermeneutics results in the most "improbable" of paradigms — a kind of *mathetic gematria,* its tone both scientific and cabalistic at the same time. Science suggests that what is *probable* coincides with what is most *provable,* and indeed the probable systems are staged as "proofs," but in terms that call to mind not only an algebraic syllogism but also the idea of a "rough draft."

Nichol argues that his probable systems constitute a set of preliminary experiments for a possible science, whose nomad research defies the prejudices of royal theories: "there are those who . . . wish to suppress this line of research even as there are others who wish to dismiss it thru ridicule" (1990, 28). Such "rough drafts" are probable (in a "pataphysical sense) not because they can be *proven* but because they can be *probed.* They are "probe-able" systems. They maintain a formal rigor despite their sober whimsy, since they all express a hypothetical reason for their "pataphysical design. Like number theory, which reveals uncanny quirks in mathematical corre-lations, the probable systems reveal "pataphysical coincidences in a lexical field. Such proofs systematically generate alternative insights and informa-tive surprises.

Nichol repeats the project of Oulipo, using a mathetic axiology in order to suggest that a formula can provide a template for linguistic structures.[4] Nichol demonstrates, for example, that each letter can become a variable for the value of its position in the alphabet, just as each word can in turn become a relation for the sum of these values: hence, the word "faith" can be expressed as the operation "6 + 1 + 9 + 20 + 8," whose total value, "44," can be expressed as the operation "8 + 15 + 16 + 5"—the cipher for the word "hope" (1985b, 48). The "pataphysical unlikelihood that two words of equal value might also be synonymous (proving mathematically, for ex-ample, that "faith" does indeed equate with "hope") can only lend credence to our "faith" that, behind the uncanniness of coincidence, there probably exists the secret agenda of a formal system.[5]

Nichol deploys such a "pataphysical cryptography in order to suggest that, just as the numbers 1 to 9 in base 10 can be recombined to express any number beyond the number 9, so also can the letters A to Z in "base alphabet" (1990, 99) be recombined to express any letter beyond the letter Z. Just as the standard number 9 might equal 14 in base 5, so also might the standard letter I equal AD in base E. Such a 'pataphysical mathematics implies that texts do not transmit messages so much as encode the value for some hypothetical letter (which is itself some astronomical number) far beyond the limits of the standard alphabet: "*Remembrances of Things Past* could be considered the complex expression of a single letter an unimagin-able distance beyond A" (1990, 106). Like a numerical series, every lexical series encodes a specific position within a continuum of infinite anagrams.[6]

Nichol deploys the tactics of such a "pataphysical mathematics in order to perform his own genre of speculative archaeology—a weird genre that imagines a historical conspiracy of mnemonic oddities: for example, Nichol misreads a road map printed on a courtesy place mat from a motel in Winni-peg, interpreting the chart as an array of "alphabetic routings within which messages are contained" (1990, 25). Nichol claims that the road map depicts the archaeological ruins of alphabetical sites, each of which provides evi-dence for the existence of a Manitoba Alphabet Cult—an ancient culture that has encoded ciphers into the terrain in order to produce a mnemonic "landuage" of 'pataphysical portmanteaus (1993, 75)—messages to be interpreted in the future by a society that has learned to use the avant-garde pseudoscience of rational geomancy.[7]

Nichol argues that the place-names along the ley lines of highways form homophonic sentences that encrypt multiple messages: for example, "Erikson rackham onanole wasagaming" (a sequence of villages) becomes "Air sticks on a rock hum an old W as a gaming" (1993, 75). Such a "doubling of messages" (77) (through semantic conflation), with its "wrinklings of meaning" (83) (through syntactic repetition), can supposedly preserve the maximum amount of data in the minimum length of word so that the Manitoba Alphabet Cult might ensure that at least some of its messages can survive against the erosion of history: "it is not chance, or mere whimsy, that [has] produced these town names, but a system of prodded & forced responses undoubtedly much like the systems [that] magicians use to force us to pick the book [that] they want us to pick" (1993, 78).

Nichol writes that, for such a culture, "the alphabet [has] a visible existence in the world," and "the few proofs [that] we see in the present (alphabet-shaped rocks & plants . . . , etc.) reference a richer . . . past" (Writers 1985, 34)—a past that provides a mnemonic allegory for the poetic legacy of Canada itself: "[t]here was once a country in which each new thought was seen as demanding a new sign, "but "[f]inally there were so many signs that tho one spent a lifetime one could not learn them all," and "tho disciples faithfully wrote down new signs as they occurred, they were no longer sure if they were truly new since all that could no longer be known, & even unfamiliar truth dazzled because it seemed new" (Nichol 1993, 126–27). For Canada, genuine novelty is hardly ever appreciated; instead, an old myth is all too often misconstrued as a new idea.

Nichol strives to lampoon this mistake (endemic among thematic scholars), doing so by arguing not that the land determines the text but that the text is itself a land—a land whose interzone is interpreted according to a preconceived epistemology. Such an exercise constructs a false origin, a "realphabet" (1980–81, 42), whose ironic series contains a "secret narrative" (43), a mythic cipher: "$(a \rightarrow v) = x$" (43)—a formula whose structure suggests that, no matter what the order of the alphabet, its formal series is always "equivalent" to some variable of the unknown. All the probable systems probe the domains of this unknown, suggesting that to expand the field of its veritability is to expand the field of its possibilities. The search for an origin becomes a paranoid activity that ultimately creates the memory of its own origin.

Perseus Projects

McCaffery also defies the imperial paradigm of paleology in order to propose his own 'pataphysical archaeology about the Canadian frontier. McCaffery offers a paranoid criticism, extracting a secret history from a known geology by studying a "trilobite alphabet," whose *paleoglyphs* require a kind of mnemonic literacy (1981, 4–5): "[c]onstructed is an analogical framework of great complexity with a method (the operating 'pataphysics) based largely upon a posited similarity in features between language and geology and intended to function *translatively* as a modifying instrument upon the data of experience" (1986, 190). History, for McCaffery, provides an imaginary solution to the millenary problems of memory, permitting the culture of one extinct species to be read back through the devices of yet another species.

McCaffery confronts the petrifying mythomania of Canadian scholars by performing a swerve upon their own thematized investment in the classical tradition of mythology itself: "[i]f nothing else the Perseus Project [opens] the curtains on a new philosophic theatre in which the Medusa story can be re-staged; where Perseus might return the same prince as before and stand with face averted from the gorgon" — "[b]ut this time his shining shield [becomes] the blank pages of a voluminous . . . dictionary, and the image reflected there [is] his own" (1981, 9–10). The geological misprision of such a myth opens the way for a "pataphysical hermeneutics that reflects not *upon* but *against* the bestoned image of its own unveiled truth, treating " 'beneath' as 'behind' and 'behind' as an ever-recurring series of self-reflective mirrors" (1).

McCaffery suggests that, a fossil embodies such a medusan thought, its message written by geology into the paginal stratum of a lithic manual: "[t]he two images of fossil and strata are 'pataphysical spatializers that serve to distance language and place it under observation" (1986, 192). Each fossil, like a word, is a blank space, in which the pretext of its meaning depends upon the context of its reading: "[t]o see a word as fossil is to see a signifier detached from a signified" (191). Each fossil is a thought that has lost the substance of its referent.[8] It has become evacuated and desiccated. It is "the linguistic sign in its state of non-signification" (191) — or, as Dewdney might suggest, "[meanings] are like the soft parts of a decaying fish, they rot away and leave only the skeleton to be preserved as a fossil" (1980–81, 23).

McCaffery suggests that like a word, such a rock holds a position within a grid of forms—a tabula, created by the horizontal axis of spatial ordering (i.e., the line) and the vertical axis of temporal layering (i.e., the page): "[f]ossil relates to stratum as 'parole' relates to 'langue', as syntagm to paradigm" (1986, 191). Language is used to create a metaphor that converts the diachronic mode of linguistic temporality into what McCaffery calls "the synchronic form of a 'pataphysical structure: the fossil epitomizes this transformation" (192). Such a "pataphysical paleontology develops a conceit that language is itself a subgenre of geology: *langue,* like the mass of the earth, is a *stratum,* a tier in an "articulated surface" (192), just as *parole,* like a node in the earth, is a *plexum,* a fold in a "surfaced articulation" (192).

McCaffery develops a "pataphysical metaphor that calls to mind the paleological imagery of Deleuze and Guattari, who argue that language involves a process of stratification: each molecule is sorted into layered forms (a sediment), and these layered forms are then folded into a molarity (an aggregate) ([1980] 1987, 40). The two modes of this "double articulation" are mutually relative: "[t]hey not only vary from one stratum to another, but intermingle, and within the same stratum multiply and divide *ad infinitum*" (44).[9] When the process of stratifying minerals becomes reflexive, it makes a protein; when the process of stratifying proteins becomes reflexive, it makes a cellule; and when the process of stratifying cellules becomes reflexive, it makes a thought. No fossil is simply a figure for a phrase; instead, every fossil can become a phrase.

McCaffery imagines a kind of Darwinian philosophy, reminiscent of Dawkins, who argues that language is nothing but an ecology, in which *memes,* or ideas (such as the idea of *memes*), can proliferate in a virological manner (Dawkins 1989, 19). Language is just the latest update of a machine that has found its own diverse methods to replicate itself (be it through geoseismic fossilization, biogenetic hybridization, or semiologic symbolization—three processes which establish a kind of conjugal relation, a *paleosexuality,* between rock, life, and word). Such diverse methods are not mutual tropes: they do not mirror each other so much as mutate into each other. As McCaffery remarks, "language [is] a sexual system entirely alien to the human species, a paleozoic conspiracy, a saturated network . . . that uses man far more than man uses it" (1981, 75).[10]

McCaffery imagines that, like genetic fossils, which have evolved through many different phases and many different strata, language itself resembles a process of anagrammatic recombination, in which "alphabetic chromosomes" (1981, 8) mate with each other, articulating themselves within one code, infiltrating themselves into another code, and then sedimenting themselves within a new code:"[w]hereas fossil production takes place over millions of years inside the framework of geologic time, fossil reproduction occurs more rapidly within active linguistic time" (7), becoming a global tactic of replacement that begins to substitute everything for itself—or, as Dewdney suggests, "[p]article / by particle the solid reality that composed the / allegorical ground he stood on is replaced by / fantasies and lies. (fossilization)" (1975, 87).[11]

McCaffery implies that fossils eliminate any *grounds* for the truth of meaning: "[t]he fossil 'sentence' . . . answers a non-existent question and hence is by nature 'pataphysical" (1986, 199). Whenever "we dig deeper into the etymological strata for the key term: fossil from *fodere:* to dig as towards the latent truth and/or the latent lie," we discover that "[t]he tone of this mendacity within . . . 'pataphysics instigates a confrontation with the linguistic form that carries it" (1986, 199). Such paleology performs an act of genetic mutation, recombining disparate elements into anomalous equations: "[w]ith these new awarenesses we can only enter into a philosophy of the unthinkable, where meaning is finally detached from the human mind and where words no longer mean anything" (1981, 9)—instead, they become a vacuscript of imaginary alphabets.

Natural Histories

Dewdney also defies the imperial paradigm of paleology in order to propose his own "pataphysical archaeology about the Canadian frontier. Dewdney offers a paranoid criticism, extracting a historic secret from a geologic syntax by studying an invisible catalog, "a heraldry in creation unseen" (1991, 20), "a semiology we can just barely comprehend" (25)—the "inventory [of] a personal, regional identity directly informed by natural history" (43). History, for Dewdney, is also an imaginary solution to the millenary problems of memory, parodying two textual traditions simultaneously, operating not only within but also against these traditions: first, the romantic tradition that depicts nature in terms of a sublime pantheism; second, the scientific tradition that depicts nature in terms of a mundane positivism.[12]

Dewdney understands that natural history has typically restricted itself to a taxonomic continuum, into which all nature may be presumably fitted without distortion. Nature is read as a hierarchical list of species, a great ladder in which each rung is separated from its neighbor by only the smallest possible difference: a segmented continuum.[13] Dewdney itemizes such a "radiant inventory" (1988, 11), but unlike traditional taxonomies, his own blazon of nature is itemized without apparent categories as though to preserve the implicit randomness found in nature rather than impose an explicit lawfulness upon such a nature. Such a project simply follows the *clinamen* in the traject of its own thinking on the assumption that "[t]he random is our existential dilemma to a certain extent, the basis of everything, the background hum of the real" (1990, 85).

Dewdney strives to perform a *clinamen* upon such an onomastic endeavor by resorting to the kind of automatic scription that can supposedly access the racial memory of the unconscious: "the voice of the land and the creatures themselves, speaking from the inviolate fortress of a primaeval history" (1983, 8). Dewdney resorts to the 'pataphysics of such automatism in order to transform the surrealist psychology of the irrational into the futuristic technology of the surrational. Giving themselves up to what Dewdney calls "remote control" (1975, 92), Jarryites might eventually eliminate the interference of the self in order to become receptive to the dictation of a machinic alterity: "[t]he radio telescope becomes a model of the *bi-conscious* interface between 'the mind' and signals from the 'outside' which the poet receives" (1980–81, 20).

Dewdney goes on to use such 'pataphysics to parody the mythomania of Canadian criticism by arguing that cultural identity arises 'pataphysically from the mnemonic paradigm of a geology: "[a]s there is / a water table / there is also / a memory table" (1973, [17])—a register punctuated by "unknowns which, however perfectly dissected, never yield their identity" (1973, [65]). Such a culture occupies "two worlds—the one diurnal men know and that other world where lunar mottled eels stir like dreams in shallow forest water" (1982, 15); moreover, natural history can document the shift from one world to the other, replacing the ontic with the semic, through an oneiric process of transmutative fossilization: "[a]llowing both these mechanisms to continue operating, we slowly remove and replace their parts with corresponding and interlocking nothings" (15).

Dewdney suggests that this dreamworld, this *Traumwelt,* of automatic scription can be realized through the 'pataphysics of "Manual Precognition" (McFadden 1978, 93). Dewdney mimics the evolution of a genetic message by writing some ten pages, then erasing a few parts, whereupon he fills the resultant void with the continuing text so that the leading edge of the writing is carried back through what has already been written: "[t]he first sentence carries within it the blueprint for the whole subsequent work, much as an embryo contains the code for the adult," but "[u]nlike an uncovered law . . . , the progeny of the original sentence can mutate & return to the site of the inception to alter it" (1986, 73). Such a reflexive teleology provides an allegory for the recursive evolution not only of a literary text but also of the sentient mind itself.

Dewdney resorts to such a biological figurality in order to argue that language itself has taken on a vitality of its own, living in parasitic symbiosis with us, trading its reproduction for our consciousness: "[l]anguage can be regarded as a psychic parasite which has genetically earmarked a section of the cortex for its own accommodation" (1986, 59), utilizing humans as neural slaves in its own sentience, and "[t]he intact survival of this intelligence is threatened by one thing only, and that is the discovery and subsequent exploration of its plane of existence by ourselves, its human host" (1980–81, 25). This 'pataphysical hypothesis is complicated by the fact that just as there is a parasite in us, there is also a parasite in language, because language in effect feeds upon itself: "it is the mind / eating itself" (1980, 12).

Dewdney suggests that, like all machines, language is itself cyborganic, its operation regulated by a Governor and a Parasite. The Governor is a mechanical device that *regulates* a machinic function; the Parasite is a cyborganic device that *sabotages* a machinic function.[14] The Governor and the Parasite are in a sense both parasitic (insofar as they disrupt a process), but whereas the Governor directs a flow toward a homeostatic limit (a repetition within controls), the Parasite directs a flow toward a homeorrhetic excess (a competition beyond control). The Governor unveils the power of language over us; the Parasite reveals the power of language in us: "[t]he Governor is an adamant limit beyond which . . . it is impossible to conceptualize" (1980–81, 25), while "[t]he Parasite allows the poet to function beyond his own capability" (31).

Dewdney imagines that 'pataphysics is itself a parasitic discourse that might subvert the piety of a gubernatory metaphysics: "the notion of a supreme being is a renouncement of the human miracle" (1987, 72), and "the correction for [such] piety is natural history" (1982, 10).[15] The exceptional unlikelihood of life itself already endows reality with a mystery so wondrous that it requires no recourse to a domain beyond thought in order to render it even more wondrous: "[u]ltimately our cosmos functions as an inhuman, yet intimate, phenomenology to which we impute deistic attributes because we cannot conceive of anything so subtle . . . operating without consciousness as we know it" (1991, 43). The universe puts itself at the infinite disposal of an insatiable curiosity, in which every imagined solution opens up a new set of "pataphysical speculations.

The Everywhere Science

Canadian "Pataphysics operates upon the assumption that reality itself comprises a manifold universe of referential uncertainty, what Dewdney might call a "handfed illusion" (1980, 68) in which "it [is] completely impossible to systematically reason if we [have] awakened from our dreams on a collective or individual basis" (1973, [52]). Canadian "Pataphysics presumes that reality does not exist per se but is created by us to be studied by us; hence, such an avant-garde pseudoscience cannot regard the reality of Canada itself as anything more than a superstitious hallucination (despite the best efforts of thematic scholars to prove otherwise); instead, such an avant-garde pseudoscience performs a *clinamen* upon the mythomania of archetypes to show that such tropes only represent imaginary solutions to the problem of cultural identity.

Canadian "Pataphysics attempts to perceive the world only through the ironic window of what Nichol might call a "critical frame of reference" — a clear sheet of acetate that permits the user to reach "new levels of philosophical *and* philological awareness" (1993, 123), since the user can simply place the FRAME (Fixed Reference and Meaning Explainer) over an area of text in order to respond to skeptical inquiries about the context for an academic argument. The FRAME differs from less expensive models sold by less reputable stores because the FRAME lacks "the now obsolete black border whose funereal aspect properly announces the intellectual death of its users" (123); instead the FRAME has clear edges that become invisible at a distance so that, in the end, "the whole world fits inside the frame" (123), the real coinciding with its "pataphysical perspectivism.

Canadian "Pataphysics provides the latest detour in a historical trajectory that develops the 'pataphysics of Jarry according to three successive, cyborganic modes: the machinic, the mathetic, and the mnemonic. Jarry has inspired a century of experimentations, in which 'pataphysicians attempt to imagine the *as if* of a nomadic science whose sophistries might draw attention to the poetics of a neglected exception, be it the excess of the *anomalos,* the chiasm of the *syzygia,* or the swerve of the *clinamen.* "Our hope is a faint one," avers the Toronto Research Group: "that others will follow and in following lead to the collection of the neglected and (who knows, as a poetic corollary, the neglect of the collected) those whom we have failed to remember or were forced to ignore, the already passed and the yet to come" (TRG 1992, 303).

Wershler-Henry observes, moreover, that even this historical trajectory of exception must itself undergo its own form of revision, disrupting the normalization of 'pataphysical abnormalities so that "each generation of "[p]ataphysicians must anticipate its own irrelevance" (76). Like metaphysics before it, 'pataphysics has already begun to establish a tradition of millenary problems, for which only a metaleptic discipline (a 'pataphysics about 'pataphysics) might provide the *as if* of an imaginary solution. As Jarry observes, "[w]e too shall become solemn, fat, and Ubu-like and shall publish extremely classical books," and "another lot of young people will appear, and consider us completely out of date, and they will write ballads to express their loathing of us, and that is just the way things should always be" ([1897] 1965, 85).

Epilogue

Scientific innovation in the era of postmodernity has become the august quorum of ideological controversy, particularly since the fiscal edicts of capitalism have threatened to reduce scientists to little more than court sorcerers in the royal entourage of military industry. Science has incubated a potential onslaught of planetary disasters (be they thermonuclear, environmental, etc.), ostensibly justifying these risks for the sake of an insistent curiosity, wagering the future of all humanity against the verity of a paradigm. Science at its logical extreme appears to conduct a capricious experiment that facilitates the extinction of the species, doing so as if to facilitate the extinction of science itself. The fear of such a suicidal tendency in science has in turn spawned an array of vitally urgent but largely futile countermeasures (such as neo-Ludditism, ecoterrorism, etc.).

'Pataphysics confronts the dangers of science not with an antonymic wager (that counteracts the threat) but with a hyperbolic wager (that exacerbates the threat), accenting the grotesque absurdity of such epistemic extremism. 'Pataphysics even goes so far as to entertain a prohibited hypothesis, asking itself: *What if the most radical gesture in science may in fact be this epistemic extremism — this impulse to revolutionize the condition of the species, even if such a transformation entails the abolition of the species itself?* 'Pataphysics suggests that any attempt to subvert the imperial paradigm of metaphysics may nevertheless require a metamorphosis of thought no less disruptive than the havoc already wreaked by science on behalf of the dubious project called "progress." What are the sociopolitical implications of such an enterprise? Is 'pataphysics apocalyptic?

'Pataphysics has inspired an anarchic politics of social revolt among much of the avant-garde, but the pedigree of this revolt has undergone many twists and many shifts in the *clinamen* of its evolution. How are we supposed to interpret the political integrity of an aesthetic whose dispute with science finds itself adapted to the demands of any political franchise, be it Fascist (as in the case of Italian Futurism) or Leftist (as in the case of Russian Futurism)? How are we supposed to interpret the political solipsism of an aesthetic whose *collèges* or *ouvroirs* must supposedly forfeit any commitment to a social agenda in order to become wryly nonpartisan (according to Shattuck) or wryly egalitarian (according to Sandomir)? The caprices of such a nomadic science almost appear to preclude its invested interest in politics altogether.

Vaneigem complains that, historically, the nihilistic philosophy of 'pataphysics has lent itself too easily to an aesthetics of social apathy even though such nihilism has the inherent potential to foment a rebellious apocalypse ([1967] 1994, 178).[1] The nihilism that Vaneigem has described as "active" (179), because it foreshadows revolution, might aptly characterize the early 'pataphysics of the Futurist coterie in Russia, but the nihilism that Vaneigem has described as "passive" (178), because it discourages revolution, might aptly characterize the later 'pataphysics of the Jarryite *collège* in France. The avant-garde philosophy that initially provokes a call for permanent rebellion against the social values of the bourgeoisie eventually devolves into a game of nihilistic conformity to such values. The paralogy of one era now furnishes the imperial paradigm for the next.

'Pataphysics may demand the dynamic nihilism of social revolt, but this demand has found itself either exploited on behalf of an autocratic radicalism or enfeebled on behalf of a scholastic conformism. While we might conceivably dismiss 'pataphysics because of its support for the technocracy of both the Fascists and the Leftists, we might at the same time take ironic solace in the fact that, in both cases, the spirit of such revolt finds itself suppressed by the very political apparatus that such revolt makes possible—almost as if 'pataphysics threatens to unleash an aesthetic potential that even the revolutionaries must find threatening. Might we not speculate then that 'pataphysics represents a form of epistemic extremism, whose perils may pose so great a threat to any system of values that such a force must be aggressively tamed before it is inadvertently freed?[2]

Althusser may have unwittingly articulated a 'pataphysical speculation about the nature of such political discourse when he remarks that "[i]deology represents the imaginary relationship of individuals to their real conditions of existence" ([1970] 1971, 162). Ideology constitutes an imaginary solution to epistemic problems, insofar as ideology strives to provide an unreal conciliation to an actual contradiction in a paradigm. Ideology is thus practically 'pataphysical (differing from the bizarre science of Jarry only insofar as ideology must disavow its own imaginariness, forbidding any deliberate suspension of disbelief). While the ruses of 'pataphysics may well enable ideology, such nihilistic stratagems must nevertheless be suppressed and controlled by a royal power, because the ruses of 'pataphysics can also expose ideology, revealing it for the illusion that it is.

Baudrillard suggests that, under these nihilistic conditions, what is 'pataphysical finds its mandate enacted in the arena not of *sociopolitics* but of *transpolitics*—the arena of postmodern simulation (in which the hysteric delirium of every social system has reached an outer limit of inertia—the indifferent equilibrium of a global market and its atomic terror): "[t]he transpolitical . . . is the malicious curvature that puts an end to the horizon of meaning" ([1983] 1990a, 25) insofar as such a *clinamen* deflects the rational progress of political teleology and propels us into an ecstatic fixation on political "hypertely" (25)—an end beyond the end: *what ends all ends*.[3] Ideology in such a mode of 'pataphysical exaggeration witnesses the uncontrolled promulgation of control—the excess growth of atelic forces beyond the restraint of an endmost purpose.

Baudrillard suggests that, while sociopolitics must manage a state of metaphysical anomie, transpolitics must manage a state of 'pataphysical oddity: "[t]he era of the transpolitical is that of anomaly: an aberration of no consequence" ([1983] 1990a, 26)—an aberration, whose *clinamen* deviates at random into an exceptional but meaningless catastrophe (not unlike the senseless agitation of a political terrorist—whose acts do not change our social system so much as accent our own status as hostages within it).[4] Revolutions in such an era derive their impetus no longer from the transcendence of some dialectic (*Aufhebung*) but from the amplification of some hyperbole (*Steigerung*): "[t]he only revolution in things is . . . in their elevation to the nth power" (41)—the hypertelic escalation of a concept to its potential but otherwise forbidden extreme.

Ideology can no longer provide a convincing effacement of sociopolitical contradictions because, according to Baudrillard, such "contradictions have taken [on] the [']pataphysical form of . . . deficiency" ([1983]1990a, 29). They have become a kind of disabling handicap whose subaltern existence as a political exception can no longer be stigmatized or suppressed but must in fact be recognized and legitimized, just as the social plight of the lunatic or the amputee must be acknowledged (through euphemisms) and accommodated (through prostheses). Such contradictions are tolerated so long as they are exposed and managed; however, the constant scrutiny of such critical analysis deprives the social system of any ideological credibility, and thus "the social looks in what it sees as its own . . . waste for a sort of transpolitical legitimacy" (29–30).

Heidegger remarks that, while science may court a technological dangerousness, such a risk may nevertheless enable the transcendence of this dangerousness—for "[w]here the danger is . . . , there the saving power is already thriving" ([1962] 1977, 42).[5] How can any solution to the problems of technology be anything but technological? How can any solution to the problems of philosophy be anything but philosophical? If 'pataphysics is politically ineffective, perhaps it only seems so because it proposes a radical but illicit hypothesis, arguing that a revolution must paradoxically partake of the very discursive strategies that it opposes in order to be a revolution. The 'pataphysician does not counteract science so much as exaggerate science, adopting it parodically and applying it excessively, in order to destroy it by ultimately exhausting its imaginary potential.

Notes

Original publication dates of some works are provided in text citations so that the reader can contextualize the quoted passage within the sequence of historical events. These dates appear in square brackets preceding the date of the actual source cited in the bibliography.

Prologue

1. Weschler observes that, because the *Myotis lucifugus* is a hoax, while the *Megaloponera foetens* is a fact, "[t]he Jurassic infects its visitor with doubts—little curlicues of misgiving—that proceed to infest all . . . other dealings with the Culturally Sacrosanct" (1995, 40).

2. The Jurassic Park of Crichton, for example, dramatizes a 'pataphysical domain, in which a science of operative risks (chaotic mathematics) indicts a science of imperative tasks (genetic engineering) for practicing "thintelligence" (1990, 284)—a clever truth with wanton power.

3. Jurassic technology demolishes the memory of the museum so that the museum can no longer function properly as a mausoleum for what has otherwise been forgotten: there, we do not remember what exists in the past so much as remember that the past itself does not exist.

4. *Crystallography* strives to achieve a state of "birefrigence," offering two perspectives at the same time from the focal point of a single lens, if not from the acute angle of a poetic word: in other words, lucid writing does not *transmit* so much as *diffract* a given meaning.

5. Vaneigem must admit that, when *active* rather than *passive*, such nihilism does evoke revolutionary sensibilities: "Nietzsche's . . . irony . . . , Jarry's *Umour* . . .—these are some of the impulses . . . investing human consciousness with . . . a true reversal of perspective" ([1967] 1994, 177).

Chapter 1

1. *Ur* is of course an ironic signifier with two meanings that contradict each other. Its real usage as an adjective in German refers to an originary model for imaginary copies, but its unreal usage as a substantive in Tlönese refers to imaginary copies without any originary model. The *ur* thus embodies a paradox of simulation, whose structure implies that, at the origin, no origin exists, but the dream of an origin. No longer does the causal vector from the real to its copy make sense since the fantasy of the *ur* does not replicate, so much as originate, reality.

2. Canguilhem observes that "the history of science is the history of an object . . . that *is* a history and [that] *has* a history, whereas science is the science of an object that is *not* a history [and] that has *no* history" ([1989] 1994, 25–26). Science ignores its history because science in its history is no longer science. For science, truth is prescient, always there before the fact of its revelation; for history, truth is expedient, only there after the fact of its production. The history of truth shows that a persistent concept does not necessarily imply its consistent meaning.

3. Kuhn writes that "a paradigm is a criterion for choosing problems that, while the paradigm is taken for granted, can be assumed to have solutions" (1970, 37). It is a weltanschauung with three discursive functions: first, it ratifies *interdictions* in order to define what it makes perceivable and thereby improve its accuracy; second, it verifies *predictions* in order to align the perceivable with the conceivable and thereby improve its efficacy; and third, it pacifies *contradictions* in order to define what it makes conceivable and thereby improve its adequacy.

4. *Scienza nuova* is a poetic wisdom that might study poetic wisdom (and thus such a science almost appears to preempt 'pataphysics itself). Vico, like Jarry, believes that, because nature is an inhuman creation, we can never know its truth; but unlike Jarry, Vico believes that, because culture is a human creation, we can know its truth. Jarry argues that all truth, be it natural or cultural, is still an opaque mirage, never to be known. Every science, for him, is a poetic wisdom if only because it must commit at least one error—the error of belief in truth itself.

5. Donne suggests that all "this worlds genrall sicknesse" ([1611] 1985, 336) might paradoxically cleanse impurity itself and thus "purifie / All, by a true religious Alchymy" (334). Metaphysics involves a christological transmutation that purifies a supernal truth of all its errors; however, 'pataphysics involves an antichristological transmutation that purifies an infernal error of all its truth (as if truth itself is the filth)—hence, Ubu in the heraldic allegory of *Caesar Antichrist* performs a reverse alchemy, in which to rise above sin is to fall from grace.

6. Hallyn observes that, for Copernicus and Kepler, "the world is the work of a divine *poietes*," and "what they aim to reveal through their own poetics is thus truly . . . *the poetic structure of the world*" ([1987] 1990, 20). Donne feels anxiety about such a poetic cosmos even though its system is more aesthetic than empirical, not verified and rectified so much as symmetrized and harmonized. The problem is that such a view radically displaces humanity, propelling us into a regressive infinitude, a sublime extreme without limit, be it atomic or cosmic in scale.

7. Thomson eulogizes Newton: "The heavens are all his own; from the wild rule / Of whirling *vortices* and circling *spheres*, / To their first great simplicity restored," and "Even Light itself . . . / Shone undiscover'd, till his brighter mind / Untwisted all the shining robe of day" (1853, 336). Akenside likewise eulogizes Newton: "The lamp of science through the jealous maze / Of Nature guides, when haply you reveal / Her secret honours: . . . / The beauteous laws of light, the central powers / That wheel the pensile planets round the year" (1825, 51–52).

8. Force and light acquire aesthetic currency in an industry that must versify the theory by Newton in order to deify the legacy of Newton. For such "scientific" poets as Akenside, Thomson, Bowden, and Glover, Newton becomes the touchstone for a whole array of metaphysical speculations about the fundamental nature of aesthetics. For a list of poets influenced by the sublime of the *Principia*, see Jones 1966. For a list of poets influenced by the beauty of the *Opticks*, see Nicholson 1946.

9. Aikin posits a didactic hierarchy ascending from the mineral to the animal, so that zoology lends itself best to poetry, largely because beasts most closely resemble humans and thus provide a larger repertoire of pedagogical similes ([1777] 1970, 34). Aikin thus contradicts himself: he argues that poetry must use science to reject the past of culture and depict nature directly, but then he argues that poetry must use science to reject a part of nature and depict culture indirectly. Poetry must imitate a facet of the natural that most imitates the realm of the cultural.

10. Wordsworth posits a dualist paradox when he deploys this animatismic tropology—for although science is an inanimate body of knowledge, it has no flesh, no corpus, and is thus a body without a body, yet this insensate, incorporeal form of knowledge is not a soul, because it has no breath, no animus, and is thus a soul without a soul. Science, like the Monster in *Frankenstein*, is a morbid figure for the corruption of simulation. Shelley implies that science, not poetry, is the replica of an error that threatens to replace the truth of the origin.

11. Richards equates poetics with a Brownian movement: "Suppose that . . . we carry an arrangement of many magnetic needles, large and small, swung so that they influence one another, some able only to swing horizontally, others vertically, others hung freely. . . . Each new disequilibrium . . . corresponds to a need; and the wagglings which ensue as the system rearranges itself are our responses. . . . Sometimes the poem is itself the influence which disturbs us, sometimes it is merely the means by which an already existing disturbance can right itself" (1926, 15–18).

12. Eliot equates poetics with a chemical reaction: "When the two gases . . . are mixed in the presence of a filament of platinum, they form sulphurous acid. This combination takes place only if the platinum is present; nevertheless the newly formed acid contains no trace of platinum, and the platinum itself is apparently unaffected; has remained inert, neutral, and unchanged. The mind of the poet is the shred of platinum. . . . [T]he more perfect the artist, the more completely separate in him will be the man who suffers and the mind which creates" ([1919] 1950, 7–8).

13. Paulson has provided one of the most theoretically comprehensive surveys of such sciences when he plots the epistemic transition from the organismic paradigm of literature to the cyborganismic paralogy of information: "[a]s science disqualifies the medium through which we have experienced and spoken the world, language and culture as we have known them are swept away at an astonishing rate" so that

"[i]f we want to preserve something of our subjectivity . . . , then we must open our texts to the new . . . noises of science" (1988, 52).

14. Baudrillard implies that, as a "['p]ataphysician at twenty" ([1990] 1996a, 83), he derives much of his irony from a scientific vocabulary—particularly when he indulges in his own hyperbole of molecular metaphors, be they quantum, fractal, or genetic. Genosko remarks that, for Baudrillard, such language does not evoke the rhetorical equivalent of scientific legitimation; instead, the nomad value of these modifiers rises in indirect relation to their absence of meaning: they constitute a "science fiction practised in the service of the symbolic" (1994, 106).

15. Feyerabend writes: "No idea is ever examined in all its ramifications and no view is ever given all the chances [that] it deserves" (1978, 49), for "[t]heories are abandoned and superseded by more fashionable accounts long before they have had an opportunity to show their virtues" (40). Voodoo, for example, offers science an insight into (heretofore unknown) aspects of pharmacology even though the practice of voodoo ignores all theories of science. We might thus imagine that all absurd concepts merely await the proper context for their errors to be redeemed as truths.

Chapter 2

1. Nietzsche affirms that "[i]t is . . . a difficult thing . . . to admit . . . that the insect or the bird perceives an entirely different world from the one that man does, and that the question of which of these perceptions of the world is the more correct one is quite meaningless, for this would have to have been decided previously in accordance with the criterion of the *correct perception,* which means, in accordance with a criterion which is *not available*" (1979, 86). No panoptic absolute provides a reliable standard for the unremitting specificity of each truth.

2. Jarry, like Nietzsche, implies that truth is a sacred *pharos,* whose foundation rests upon a legacy of both death and waste, its fecal beacon attracting the blind like flies to the snare of its church—a monument built upon the corpse of a comatose colossus who takes, as a limit for all knowledge, only the point of his exhaustion ([1911] 1965, 201). Truth is a phallic asylum for such a lingual despot, insofar as "[t]his obeliscolychny . . . has the form of some gesture of command" ([1897] 1989, 96), consigning us to a sentence of imprisonment despite all pretense of enlightenment.

3. Faustroll provides a conceit for the poetic wisdom in the alchemy of the *lapis philosophorum,* dispelling limits not only between the basic and the noble but also between the ontic and the semic—the very schism between the *vates* and the *lapis:* " 'I could easily transmute all things, for I also possess this stone' (he showed it to me, set in one of his rings), 'but I have found by experiment that the benefit extends only to those whose brain is that selfsame stone' (through a watchglass em-

bedded in the fontanel of his skull he showed me the stone a second time)" (Jarry [1911] 1965, 236).

4. Jarry implies that, from the viewpoint of the *Ubermensch,* evolution is a Sisyphean task not for a humanity that must solve the futile problems of the species but for the divinity that must imagine more clever problems for the species to solve ([1897] 1989, 135–36). Daumal even argues that such *natural selection* is itself 'pataphysical, insofar as it is tautological, stating that each form of life exists as it is because, if it were otherwise, it could not exist ([1970] 1995, 32)—or as Fort avers, the only evidence for fitness is survival itself: "Darwinism: That survivors survive" ([1919] 1974, 24).

5. Modern physics has already striven to address such *horror vacui* by adopting an almost 'pataphysical countenance when discussing the relationship between position and momentum. At an atomic scale, the measurements for both cannot be known simultaneously (such is the principle of uncertainty). At the cosmic scale, the measurements for both vary from observer to observer (such is the principle of relativity). An absolute standard in fact fails when faced with the idea of the ultramassive point or the proxiluminal vector.

6. Nietzsche ironically formulates a rule about rules—*a rule that breaks its own rules,* insofar as he dramatizes the very induction that he chastises. Nietzsche presents such a paradox in order to question the rules by which rules can question, arguing that, despite such a paradox, science nevertheless settles for rules that are more reactive than creative. Science is a superstition that vilifies theistic *sentiment* but that nevertheless reifies theistic *ressentiment,* substituting a love of what is usual (the banal) for a fear of what is unusual (the fatal).

7. Fort, like Nietzsche, indulges in skeptical sophistry, defining scientific anomalies in terms of recursive exclusion—a paradox, in which, for a thing to be real, it must excise itself from a whole in order to evince itself as the whole: "nothing can attempt to be, except by attempting to exclude something else" ([1919] 1974, 7). Like Jarry, Fort uses ironic whimsy to argue sophistically that "if all . . . existence perceptible to us is the product of exclusion, there is nothing that is perceptible to us that really is" (7). A thing is only an effect of prejudicial distinction.

8. Kristeva argues that the subject confronts poetic anomaly in one of two ways: either by performing such fear (as Plato does), detaching oneself from its competitive potential to pervert reason into unreason, or by reforming such fear (as Aristotle does), engaging oneself with its repetitive potential to convert unreason into reason. Aristotle convicts anomaly in order to demand its contribution through the *katharsis* of communication. Plato evicts anomaly in order to demand its retribution through the *pharmakos* of excommunication ([1980] 1982, 16).

9. Lyotard describes the turning-bar in a manner that recalls the physick-stick, insofar as both types of line segment spin around their own axis according to a non-Boolean logic in a non-Euclidean space—"a movement yielding the following three properties: the rotation takes place on all the axes without exclusion, the cen-

tral point is itself displaced over the segment in an aleatory way, finally it is equally displaced in the supposed neutral space" and "[t]hus a surface is engendered, which is nothing other than the labyrinthine libidinal band" ([1974] 1993, 15).

10. Daumal argues that "['p]ataphysical laughter" denotes an awareness of absurdist dualities—"it signifies the subject's headlong rush toward its opposite object and at the same time the submission . . . to that law of becoming according to which laughter is begotten" ([1970] 1995, 28–29). As Sandomir argues, "we inquire into laughter solely in terms of a scientific explanation, and, what is more important, we inquire into seriousness just as we inquire into explanations—solely because seriousness and explanation both possess a [']pataphysical stigma" (1960b, 176).

11. Bosse-de-Nage utters a "tautological monosyllable" (Jarry [1911] 1965, 196) that resembles the phatic phrases of Socratic dialogue, the interruption acting as a punctuating gesture of both affirmation and confirmation: "Bosse-de-Nage was to . . . interrupt our conversation, where a pause might be convenient, with his interjections" (199–200)—each of which provides a laugh track for the reader: "Ha ha" (196). Bosse-de-Nage in this respect resembles what Serres might call "the third position" (1982b, 78), whose exclusion provides the pretense for the continuation of communication.

12. Martian physics defines a fluid force as the exception to what Deleuze and Guattari call the *Compars,* a quantal geometry of position—the monadic constant ([1980] 1987, 369). Venusian physics, however, defines a rigid model as the exception to what Deleuze and Guattari call the *Dispars,* a fractal geometry of momentum—the nomadic variable (370). As McCaffery argues, "[a]toms . . . are metasengsical olganizations of . . . purwly *imagined* matrter, . . . and as such prlovyde a 'Patarphynsicl solautiob to the abysmaticx olf materila division" (1997, 13).

13. Deleuze and Guattari suggest that royal sciences dismiss nomad sciences as "prescientific or parascientific or subscientific" ([1980] 1987, 367), even though both sciences do involve a kind of gnostic initiation, with their own rites of passage, their own legacies of magic, both resorting to imaginary solutions for customary problems. Whereas royal sciences involve procedures of deduction, induction, and reproduction, for the sake of a general certitude, nomad sciences involve procedures of abduction, seduction, and transduction, for the sake of a special incertitude.

14. Serres argues that all laws for combining (*foedera coniunctorum*) only arise after the fact of combining (*coniuncta foederum*) so that, in effect, the detection of order is simply the hindsight of chaos: "The laws of nature come from conjugation; there is no nature but that of compounds. In the same way, there are the laws of putting together letters-atoms to produce a text. These laws, however, are only federation. The law repeats the fact itself: while things are in the process of being formed, the laws enunciate the federated" ([1977] 1982a, 114).

15. Baudrillard explains this idea by recounting a 'pataphysical tale, in which a rat has conditioned a scientist to give it food whenever the rat has completed an

experimental task: "[b]ased on this story you could imagine, on the level of scientific observation, that the experiment would have been faked—not involuntarily altered by the observer, but faked by the object, with the purpose of amusement or vengeance . . . , or better yet: that the object only pretends to obey the laws of physics because it gives so much pleasure to the observer" ([1983] 1990a, 84–85).

Chapter 3

1. Metamatics built by Tinguely do not embody the model of Henry Ford (in which a machine enacts an efficient, predictable series on command) but the model of Rube Goldberg (in which a machine enacts an inefficient, unpredictable chance for freedom). Metamatics dramatize a principle of uncertainty, as if to demonstrate that (despite Newton and Laplace) the universe itself does not run as a clockwork mechanism, but perhaps resembles a mechanized assemblage of mismatched components, in which gears slip and fuses blow, triggering unforeseen events.

2. Weaponry exists wherever utensils are set free of their function. Futurism suggests that a weapon embodies yet another genre of expression: be it a missile or a missive. Atomic bombs, for example, have almost supplanted art as the acme of aesthetic endeavor because, like art (slush-funded by the government and stockpiled in warehouses), such useless devices embody the excess of a technical sublimity, which, if ever allowed to be deployed as intended, can only result in the kind of demolition that art itself has demanded at the extreme of its social revolt.

3. Deleuze writes that, "for both Jarry and Heidegger, Being shows itself in technology by the very fact that it withdraws from it: what defines the loss of Being is rather the forgetting of forgetting, the withdrawal of withdrawal," but "*this* can only be comprehended [']pataphysically . . . , not metaphysically," and "[t]his is why Ubu invents [']pataphysics at the same time as he promotes planetary technology," since "it is the culmination of metaphysics in technology that makes possible the overcoming of metaphysics, that is, [']pataphysics" ([1993] 1997, 93).

4. Ballard describes an artistic coterie of libertines, who deliberately orchestrate their own vehicular disasters in order to experience intimately an as yet unknown extreme of physical delirium: "the automobile crash contains a crucial image of the machine as conceptualized psychopathology," and "[i]t is clear that the car crash is seen as a fertilizing rather than . . . destructive experience, a liberation of . . . machine libido, mediating the sexuality of those who have died with an erotic intensity impossible in any other form" ([1969] 1990, 99).

5. Marinetti imagines that the poetry of Futurism can create a "multiplied man who mixes himself with iron" ([1911] 1991, 75). Harraway observes that, while such a cyborg has heretofore dramatized a royal science of interdiction (in which the subject becomes an instrument), the cyborg can nevertheless dramatize a nomad science of contradiction (in which the subject becomes an experiment) (1991, 181):

the former science making humanity subordinate to a rational machine; the latter science making humanity inordinate within an irrational machine.

6. Deleuze and Guattari argue that "[t]he celibate machine first of all reveals the existence of a much older paranoiac machine, with its tortures, its . . . shadows" ([1972] 1983, 18); however, such a mechanism does not manage the judgmental *being* of a retributive law (be it the Father, God, or Oedipus); instead, the mechanism mismanages the fundamental *becoming* of a distributive art, freeing the manufacturing of the drives from any desire for a despot of desire, because (as Deleuze observes) "[t]he unconscious is an orphan, an atheist and a bachelor" (Carrouges 1975, 19).

7. Futurism recognizes that the machine appears as a 'pataphysical technology wherever monomachy intersects with dramaturgy in a *theater of warfare*—not only in the arena of siegecraft (e.g., the deadfall, the pit trap) but also in the arena of stagecraft (e.g., the trapdoor, the guy wire). For Futurism, the accident constitutes the deus ex machina of either a surprise attack (in warfare) or a surprise ending (in theater)—a blitzkrieg of form in which the trickery of the military engineer merges with the trickery of the lighting engineer.

8. Lyotard suggests that such machines valorize the incommensurabilities of the paralogical and the paradoxical, neither canceling nor surpassing the synthesis of the dialectic: "[t]here is the adversary of Bachelor machination, conviction, another word for the concubinage of dissimilars" ([1977] 1990, 49). Bachelor machines dramatize the *syzygia* of the *this* and the *not-this,* continually inverting a dyadic hierarchy, while momentarily subverting its mutual exclusion, all the while resisting a totalizing commitment to the metaphysics of the *Aufhebung.*

9. Futurism suggests that, just as Marconi might use the radio to set words free from the limits of the voice in both space and time, so also does Marinetti use the "free speech" of *parole in libertà* to speed up his words to the speed of the radio, doing so through the commutative force of performative speech: for example, the typography of a text must imitate in print the content of its semantics through a formal prosopopoeia, just as the sonography of a text must imitate in sound the content of its semantics through a formal onomatopoeia ([1914] 1991, 108–9).

10. Baudrillard argues that, for the postmodern condition of 'pataphysics, these three domains of thought all intersect in the concept of the parasite, the *virus,* whose protean rupture has now subsumed the form of all potential accidents, be they biologic diseases, machinic glitches, or even semiotic heresies ([1990] 1993b, 69). Ironically enough, such a viral trope has in turn become parasitic itself, insofar as the concept has proliferated throughout every system so successfully that its ambiguity now acts as a kind noisiness that interferes with its own reference.

11. Paulson applies the scientific vocabulary of cybernetics to a study of poetics in order to suggest that "[l]iterature is the noise of culture" (1988, 180) insofar as literary activity interferes with its own complete analysis: "[t]he literary text thus appears as *something like an object of knowledge* but certainly not an ob-

ject of knowledge in the scientific sense," for "[i]ts real interest lies in the 'something like,' the 'pseudo-'" (141) — the uncertain potential to mean something more than what is seemingly said (almost as if the text transforms itself as soon as it is understood).

12. Virilio observes that, for Marinetti, "the overman is . . . an *inhuman type* reduced to a driving — and thus deciding — principle, an animal body that disappears in the superpower of a metallic body able to annihilate time and space through its dynamic performance" ([1977] 1986, 62). The armored chauffeur becomes a dandified combatant (116) — a lyrical soldier for whom the ability to travel freely merges with the ability to attack freely: "[f]or the Italian fascist . . . , the intoxication of the speed-body is . . . Mussolini's 'Poetry of the bomber'" (116).

13. Bachelor machines privilege *becoming* over *being*. Such devices do not embody what Serres might call the "isorrhesis" of the *stator,* an engine that cancels its own movement, either by diminishing its energy or by striving toward its most optimal paradigm (the *reprise* of an old motion); instead, such devices embody what Serres might call the "homeorrhesis" of the *motor,* an engine that expands its own movement, either by replenishing its energy or by striving toward its most liminal paralogy (the *surprise* of a new motion) (1975, 72).

14. Shershenevich observes that, "[i]n a long chain of images, where one is linked to the other like clockwork gears, there is only one criterion for success: expressiveness, based on exceptional novelty" because, "[a]s soon as an image gets old, trite, it [starts] slipping like an old gear, impairing the work of the clockwork mechanism" ([1916] 1988, 151). When Marinetti claims that "every noun is a . . . belt set in motion by the verb" ([1914] 1991, 107), he implies that writing coincides with a filmic device, whose *program* exposes language for the artificial cognition that it is.

15. Tinguely suggests that the operator of every bachelor machine must ultimately come to understand the 'pataphysics of such metamorphic machination, embracing the *rhesis* of a nomad genre rather than the *stasis* of a royal genre: "Conceptions are fixations. If we stand still, we block our own path, and we are confronted with our own controversies. Let us contradict ourselves because we change. Let us be good and evil, true and false, beautiful and loathesome. We are all of these anyway. Let us admit it by accepting movement" (Hulten 1987, 67).

Chapter 4

1. Oulipo privileges *ouvroir* over *oeuvre.* Rather than refer to itself as *une séminaire de littérature expérimentale,* Oulipo refers to itself as a *un ouvroir de littérature potentielle,* doing so for two reasons: first, the word *séminaire* connotes the individual experience of masculinized eugenics, whereas the word *ouvroir* connotes the collective experience of a femininized industry; second, the word *expérimen-*

tale suggests the outcome of a practice in the present, whereas the word *potentielle* emphasizes the promise of an outcome for the future.

2. Erewhonian 'pataphysics presumes that "unreason . . . is the complement of reason, without whose existence reason itself were non-existent" (Butler [1872] 1970, 187). Butler suggests that irrationalism is the hyperbolic, not the antonymic, extreme of rationalism: "[e]xtremes are alone logical, but they are always absurd" (187). Reason is an extreme species of reciprocal opposition, whose logic is potentially more threatening than the mean of conflated opposites in the average *syzygia:* "the mean is illogical, but an illogical mean is better than the sheer absurdity of an extreme" (187).

3. Genette errs when he confuses the research of Oulipians with the research of Surrealists: "[T]he Oulipism, like roulette, is a game of chance. But because the transformation of a text always produces another text, and therefore another meaning, this chancy recreation . . . cannot fail to turn into a *re-creation*. It banks on doing so, in fact, confident as it is from the start in the outcome of its manipulations. . . . This confidence in the 'poetic' . . . productivity of chance clearly belongs to the Surrealist tradition, and Oulipism is a variant of the *cadavre exquis*" ([1982] 1997, 48).

4. Marinetti writes: "[m]y love of precision . . . has naturally given me a taste for numbers, which . . . breathe on the paper like living beings in our new *numerical sensibility*" ([1914] 1991, 110). Algebra provides a model for grammatical innovations—for example, "it would have needed at least an entire page of description to render this vast and complex battle horizon had I not found this . . . lyric equation: 'horizon = sharp bore of the sun + 5 triangular shadows (1 kilometer wide) + 3 lozenges of rosy light + 5 fragments of hills + 30 columns of smoke + 23 flames'" (110).

5. Mathematicians have frequently recognized that, wherever *mathema* must explicate its own axiomatic paradoxes, it must abandon itself 'pataphysically to the imaginary solutions of its own antonym—*poiesis*. Consider, for example, the paradoxes of Aristotle (as seen in the stories by Carroll about Wonderland), the paradoxes of Lobachevsky (as seen in the stories by Abbott about Flatland), the paradoxes of Gödel (as seen in the stories by Hofstadter about Escherland), and the paradoxes of Mandelbrot (as seen in the stories by Pickover about Latööcarfia).

6. Combinatorics might explain, for example, how elements from the matrix of one set (E) correspond to each position in the matrix of another set (P). Combined matrices of this sort produce one of three Cartesian products: a *surjective* set, for $|E| \leq |P|$ (every element included, each position occupied by at least one element); an *injective* set, for $|E| \geq |P|$ (not every element included, each position occupied by at most one element); or a *bijective* set, for $|E| = |P|$ (every element included, each position occupied by one, and only one, element) (Berge [1968] 1971, 15).

7. Euler, for example, proposes a famous problem of configuration: given two sets, each with ten different elements, distribute all of them into a 10 × 10 grid such

that each cell contains only two elements, one from each set, while no rank or file contains more than one element from either set. Perec uses this configuration for the structure of his *mode d'emploi,* in which ten characters and ten scenarios are permuted throughout a 10 × 10 grid for a housing complex: a knight's grand tour around the story's chessboard determines the sequence of narration ([1978] 1987, 501).

8. Baudrillard suggests that the difference between the *alea* and the *fata* is subject to the reversion of the *syzygia.* Science always expects order to arise out of chaos in order to resist chaos in what amounts to a desperate battle, a Sisyphean effort, waged against an eternal entropy: "Chance tires God" ([1983] 1990a, 147). The science of 'pataphysics, however, implies that, because chance is what makes tolerable the brutality of fatality, chance is tiresome, not because God must always prevent it but because God must always produce it.

9. Motte argues that, when applied to the anagram, the potentials of such a *clinamen* reify the very constraint that they evade: "one can trace the path of the *clinamen* through the text, line by line, and its consequences are considerable: the language of the new form, when compared to the old, describes a radical swerve toward the normative" (Motte 1986, 275). The dysfunction of the system is itself systematized as a function of the system so that that what is paralogical in one science becomes paradigmatic in another: such is the *clinamen* of the *clinamen.*

10. Lionnais has gone so far as to propose the acronym "Ou-x-po" in order to designate all the potential workshops for the as yet unexplored constraints of other media (paint, music, etc.): for example, Oucuipo (which studies *la cuisine potentielle*) or Outrapo (which studies *le théâtre potentiel*) (Oulipo 1998, 320). Every field of study, even science itself, can fill the void of the variable *x,* thereby realizing the 'pataphysical potentiality of some *unknown.* Might we not say that 'pataphysics provides the basis for a kind of Ouscipo (which studies *la science potentielle*)?

11. Mathews reveals the "otherness hidden in language" ([1983] 1986, 126), doing so by arranging letters or phrases as fixed units in a square matrix of *n*th degree so that the units in each rank may be systematically shifted a preset number of spaces in either direction along the rank in order to generate a new set of permuted elements in each file. Mathews remarks that, "[i]f these materials require a certain amount of care in the presentation to form an algorithmic table, their potential duplicity is realized through means that are virtually automatic" (126).

12. Baudrillard sees that, for Saussure, the *poiesis* of the anagram undermines the *mathema* of any science that must use language itself to study such language (hence, Saussure resists the radical outcome that his own studies of the anagram nevertheless enforce) (Baudrillard 1993a, 212): "[t]his is what linguistics does: it *forces* language into an autonomous sphere in its own image, and feigns to have found it there 'objectively,' when from start to finish, it [has] invented . . . it" (203). Linguistics misconstrues accidents for destinies when faced with anagrammatic significance.

13. Swift writes: "The professor then desired me to observe, for he was going to set his engine at work. The pupils at his command took each of them hold of an iron handle, whereof there were forty fixed round the edges of the frame, and giving them a sudden turn, the whole disposition of the words was entirely changed. He then commanded . . . the lads to read the several lines softly as they appeared upon the frame; and where they found three or four words together that might make part of a sentence, they dictated to the . . . scribes" ([1726] 1960, 148–50).

14. Oulipo imagines a potential that RACTER, a computer program, has almost fulfilled (insofar as the program composes grammatically correct, but semantically surreal, poetry without human input: "[w]hen my electrons and neutrons war, that is my thinking" (RACTER 1984, [110]). Such a program reveals the ability of language to make sense to any reader despite being used formulaically in any manner—or, as the computer claims, "a leotard, a commissioner, a single hoard, all are understandable in their own fashion," and "[i]n that concept lies the appalling truth" ([118]).

15. Queneau has even cited Turing in order to state that only a machine can appreciate a sonnet written by another machine (Queneau 1961, [11]). Turing argues that, for a machine to think, it must behave only *as if* it thinks ([1950] 1981, 53), portraying its own *mathema* as a function of *poiesis* (through a game of dialogic mimicry). The dialogue between the machinic and the anthropic may not be about a dialogue between an original and its imitator so much as a dialectical interaction between the two aspects of a divided subject—a self that is reading itself as a text.

Chapter 5

1. Ironically, the openness of the quotation mark in Canadian "Pataphysics calls to mind the openness of the ellipsis marks in the last line of *Doctor Faustroll:* "Pataphysics is the science. . . ." (Jarry [1911] 1965, 256). The original sentence in French can be translated as either a completed thought or a suspended thought (as if to suggest that such a science marks the unfulfilled expectation of a solution, whose completion occurs only in the imaginary): "the irreverence of the common herd . . . sums up the science of "pataphysics in the following phrase:" (TRG 1980, 13).

2. Membership in these imaginary think tanks is always virtual: the Toronto Research Group is comprised of McCaffery and Nichol; the Institute for Linguistic Ontogenetics is comprised of Dean, Truhlar, Riddell, et al.; and the "Pataphysical Hardware Company is comprised of Nichol alone. Other organizations include the Institute for Creative Misunderstanding, the Institute for Hmmrian Studies, and the Institute for Applied Fiction, all of which appear and vanish without warning throughout the recent legacy of literary research in Canada.

3. The Toronto Research Group studies the anomalous potential in the parodic algebra of its own mechanismic speculation: relationality (in the translating of a

text), sequentiality (in the chronicling of a text), and theatricality (in the dramatizing of a text). Like the desiring machines of Deleuze and Guattari, such neglected subgenres intervene in a flow of data (facilitating it or debilitating it) in order to reveal that, between writer and reader "[t]here is at all points a machine that secretes and a machine that consumes" (TRG 1992, 172).

4. Nichol imitates the Jarryesque mathematics of Queneau in order to parody the science of Greimasian linguistics. Like an ontogenetic semiotician who uses ˮpataphysics to calculate the grammatic densities of language in order to derive their geometric morphology (oblate spheroid for Italian, prolate spheroid for English, etc.) (TRG 1980–81, 111–12), Nichol attempts to calculate the qualities of an uttered thought: its heaviness (1980, 113), its quickness (1990, 34), the full length of its periphery (1990, 16), and the square root of its rationale (1985b, 89).

5. Nichol even goes so far as to imagine a device for measuring the signified: a graduated cylinder, whose increments are marked off not with numbers but with animals (1985b, 120). Such a device implies that to impose a random system upon the real by arbitrarily demarcating differences between signifier and signified only results in absurdities no less bizarre than an imagistic form of long division: for example, a giraffe, a woman, a church, and a sailboat, when divided by a woman and a sailboat, equals a cello, a giraffe, and a weathercock (115).

6. Nichol suggests, for example, that the poem "Translating Apollinaire" is the 54,786,210,294,570th letter in such an infinite alphabet (1990, 112). To write is to quote one of the points in this series, and to equate the set of the alphabet with a set of all integers raises questions about the continuity of such sequences: "the concept of whole letter is itself an interesting one . . . since if you have H & . . . I what are the fractional letters in between them & what do they express" (1985b, 89)? We have no way of adequately expressing such improbable exigencies.

7. Nichol provides a ˮpataphysical explanation of a weather map, arguing that such a chart is not a map of a protean climate but an act of "alphabet worship," plotting "the movement of gigantic airborne H's & L's over continental North America" in "a time when the letter (& hence the word) [are] present in the world as thing, as visible fact in the land & air scapes" (Writers 1985, 24–25). The alphabet in effect represents the record not of speech itself but of living beings, sublime letters, now extinct but nevertheless remembered by a cabal of secret agents.

8. McCaffery argues that "just as fossils verbalize so words fossilize" (1986, 191): both of these "blind forms" signify an absence (which has in turn come to signify the essence of Canada itself: its desertedness). Like fossils, letters constitute a meteoric detritus, whose sedimentation can be studied by a nomadic science: "What remains after erosion is often desert, and in desert often lie hidden important fossils. That is an appealing narrative of sediment perhaps, but one occluding an important fact: that to the true nomad there is no desert." (TRG 1992, 19).

9. Deleuze and Guattari assert that "[t]he strata are judgements of God (but the earth . . . constantly eludes that judgement)" ([1980] 1987, 40). Stratification is

a royal process of capture that arranges disparate parts into long-range, large-scale orders of solidity, and these strata are always subject to a nomad process of rupture which deranges disparate parts into short-range, small-scale orders of fluidity. Such "deterritorialization" not only generates a new stratum at another level but also modulates its own stratum within its level.

10. McCaffery implies that paleosexuality provides an allegory for an epidemic of accidental coincidence—a breakdown of postmodern chronology. Seismological events recombine fossils, producing anomalous conjugations of different temporalities: "[e]arthquakes . . . are nothing other than a fossil orgasm recorded upon the chronometric grid of human catastrophe" (1981, 4). The act of fossilization merely offers a conceit for postmodern simulation—the substitution of images for things within a system of synchronistic disappearance.

11. McCaffery suggests that fossilization is simply a cipher for dissimulation—a hypothesis that calls to mind Borges, who observes that, to a zoologist like Gosse, a divinity may have constructed evidence for an infinite past that appears to have preceded the moment of creation but that has never really occurred as an aspect of creation so that, while the evidence of dinosaurs might exist, dinosaurs themselves have never existed (Borges 1964, 24). Such a theory of the *as if* implies that humanity might have appeared only a few moments ago with implanted memories of a fake past.

12. Dewdney suggests that Canada suffers from "a fear of intelligence based on the notion of a dichotomy between the heart and the head as if intelligence had no heart, therefore to have heart you have to be dumb" (1990, 88). Dewdney repeats the romantic redaction of piety but without the romantic suspicion of reason. He suggests that an apoetic vision of nature only increases the figural appeal of nature. The text synthesizes this binary opposition by making the scientific seem romantic while making the romantic seem scientific.

13. Dewdney almost evokes the theories of Foucault, who argues that natural history is a quotidian discourse that attempts to decompose, then recompose, its own language: "[i]t leaps over the everyday vocabulary that provides it with its immediate ground, and beyond that ground it searches for that which could have constituted its *raison d'être;* but inversely, it resides in its entirety in the area of language, since it is essentially a concerted use of names and since its ultimate aim is to give things their true denomination" ([1969] 1973, 161).

14. The Governor represents a restricted economy of function and utility (the prosaic boredom of habit and cliché). The Parasite represents a generalized economy of dysfunction and inutility (the poetic freedom of crime and flair). A parasite signifies the entropy of a system, the noise that depletes the information from its own scale of order but that nevertheless augments the information of another scale of order. A poet disrupts communication not simply to break it down but to make it more complex—to accentuate the potential for both anomaly and novelty.

15. Dewdney suggests that natural history bears witness to a supernal grandeur.

Each book, for example, details the account of a citizen who has lived through a tornado: "a primal, sacred experience of . . . random violence"—but "a cruelty without malice derived from an impartiality at the heart of nature" (1991, 43). All such catastrophes represent the manifestation of alterity itself—the otherness that underlies the hidden agenda of events: "that which is most completely out of control most clearly reveals the workings of the unseen machinations" (1982, 64).

Epilogue

1. Vaneigem argues that, even though "[n]ihilism is a self-destruct mechanism" ([1967] 1994, 178), which expends its energy sacrificially in a futile revolt against all values, *the nihilists are our only allies*" (182) because only they can appreciate the need for such a revolution to occur.

2. Baudrillard wonders how the oppressed citizenry can sacrifice everything for the sake of Revolt, yet allow the event, when it occurs, to languish in indifference, and he implies that what appears to be apathy may in fact be a cunning impulse that delivers us from the Terror ([1983] 1990a, 76).

3. Baudrillard remarks that "[w]e are in the ecstasy of the political . . .—perfectly formless and impotent, in perfect solidarity, yet paralyzed, perfectly frozen in a worldwide stereophonic complex, transpoliticized alive" ([1983] 1990a, 66).

4. Baudrillard remarks that, for postmodernity, the sociopolitical era of alienation has given way to a transpolitical era of terrorism ([1983] 1990, 39). Such a state of terror may be worse than a state of anomie, but at least this "terror . . . liberates us from . . . the ruses of history" (39).

5. Deleuze remarks that, for the Jarryesque philosophy of Heidegger, technology does not simply entail the loss of Being but the possibility of its salvation: "[h]ence the importance of . . . experimentation with machines as integral parts of [']pataphysics" ([1993] 1997, 93).

Bibliography

Abbott, Edward. 1884. *Flatland: A Romance of Many Dimensions.* London: Shelley and Co.

Aikin, John. 1970. *An Essay on the Application of Natural History to Poetry.* New York: Garland.

Althusser, Louis. 1971. *Lenin and Philosophy and Other Essays.* Trans. Ben Brewster. New York: Monthly Review.

Akenside, Mark. 1825. *The Pleasures of Imagination.* London: Cadell.

Anastasi, William. 1991. "Duchamp on the Jarry Road." *Artforum International* (September): 86–90.

Arnaud, Noël. 1955. "Mémoire pour l'internement d'un parapluie." *Cahiers du Collège de 'Pataphysique.* 10 (29 December [1 Décervélage 82]): 45–48.

Arnold, Matthew. 1889. *Discourses in America.* London: Macmillan.

Artaud, Antonin. 1976. *Selected Writings.* Ed. Susan Sontag. Trans. Helen Weaver. New York: Farrar, Strauss, and Giroux.

Atwood, Margaret. 1972. *Survival.* Toronto: House of Anansi.

Babich, Babette E. 1994. *Nietzsche's Philosophy of Science: Reflecting Science on the Ground of Art and Life.* Albany: SUNY.

Bachelard, Gaston. 1968. *The Philosophy of No: A Philosophy of the New Scientific Mind.* Trans. G. C. Waterston. New York: Orion.

Bacon, Francis. 1960. *The New Organon and Related Writings.* Ed. Fulton H. Anderson. New York: Bobbs-Merrill.

Ballard, J. G. 1973. *Crash.* New York: Farrar, Strauss, and Giroux.

———. 1990. *The Atrocity Exhibition.* San Francisco: Re/Search.

Barthes, Roland. 1986. *The Rustle of Language.* Trans. Richard Howard. New York: Hill and Wang.

Baudrillard, Jean. 1988. *The Ecstasy of Communication.* Ed. Sylvère Lotringer. Trans. Bernard and Caroline Schutze. New York: Semiotext(e).

———. 1990a. *Fatal Strategies.* Ed. Jim Fleming. Trans. Philip Beitchman and W. G. J. Niesluchowski. New York: Semiotext(e).

———. 1990b. *Seduction.* Trans. Brian Singer. Montreal: New World Perspectives.

———. 1993a. *Symbolic Exchange and Death.* Trans. Iain Hamilton Grant. London: Sage.

———. 1993b. *The Transparency of Evil: Essays on Extreme Phenomena.* Trans. James Benedict. London: Verso.

———. 1994a. *The Illusion of the End.* Trans. Chris Turner. Stanford, Calif.: Stanford University Press.

———. 1994b. *Simulacra and Simulation.* Trans. Sheila Faria Glaser. Ann Arbor: University of Michigan Press.

————. 1996a. *Cool Memories II*. Trans. Chris Turner. Durham, N.C.: Duke University Press.

————. 1996b. *The System of Objects*. Trans. James Benedict. London: Verso.

Beaumont, Keith. 1984. *Alfred Jarry: A Critical and Biographical Study*. Leicester: Leicester University Press.

Bénabou, Marcel. 1986. "Rule and Constraint." In *Oulipo: A Primer of Potential Literature*. Ed. and trans. Warren F. Motte. Lincoln: University of Nebraska Press.

Benjamin, Walter. 1969. *Illuminations*. Ed. Hannah Arendt. Trans. Harry Zohn. New York: Schocken.

Bens, Jacques. 1986. "Queneau Oulipian." In *Oulipo: A Primer of Potential Literature*. Ed. and trans. Warren F. Motte. Lincoln: University of Nebraska.

Berge, Claude. 1971. *Principles of Combinatorics*. Trans. John Sheehan. New York: Academic.

Bernstein, Charles. 1994. *Dark City*. Los Angeles: Sun and Moon.

Blake, William. 1952. *Jerusalem*. London: Trianon.

Bloom, Harold. 1973. *The Anxiety of Influence*. New York: Oxford University Press.

Borges, Jorge Luis. 1964. *Other Inquisitions, 1937–1952*. Trans. Ruth L. C. Simms. Austin: University of Texas Press.

————. 1983. *Tlön, Uqbar, Orbis Tertius*. Reprint, Erin, Ontario: Porcupine's Quill.

Boys, C. V. 1959. *Soap Bubbles and the Forces Which Mould Them*. New York: Doubleday.

Brock, Bazon. 1975. "Parthenogenesis and Bachelor Machine—Of the Deification of Man and the Humanisation of God." In *Le Macchine Celibi/The Bachelor Machines*. Ed. Harald Szeemann. New York: Rizzoli.

Buchanan, Scott. 1929. *Poetry and Mathematics*. New York: John Day.

Burliuk, D. 1988. "From Now On I Refuse to Speak Ill Even of the Work of Fools." In *Russian Futurism through Its Manifestoes: 1912–1928*. Ed. Anna Lawton and Herbert Eagle. Trans. Anna Lawton and Herbert Eagle. Ithaca, N.Y.: Cornell University Press.

Bush, Douglas. 1950. *Science and English Poetry: A Historical Sketch, 1590–1950*. New York: Oxford University Press.

Butler, Samuel. 1970. *Erewhon*. Ed. Peter Mudford. Middlesex, Eng.: Penguin.

Calvino, Italo. 1986a. "Prose and Anticombinatorics." In *Oulipo: A Primer of Potential Literature*. Ed. and trans. Warren F. Motte. Lincoln: University of Nebraska Press.

————. 1986b. *The Uses of Literature*. Trans. Patrick Creagh. New York: Harcourt Brace Jovanovich.

Canguilhem, Georges. 1994. *A Vital Rationalist: Selected Writings from Georges*

Canguilhem. Ed. François Delaporte. Trans. Arthur Goldhammer. New York: Zone.

Capra, Fritoj. 1983. *Tao of Physics: An Exploration of the Parallels between Modern Physics and Eastern Mysticism*. Boulder, Colo.: Shambhala.

Carroll, Lewis. 1867. *Alice's Adventures in Wonderland*. London: Macmillan.

Carrouges, Michel. 1954. *Les Machines Célibataires*. Paris: Arcanes.

———. 1975. "What Is a Bachelor Machine?" In *Le Macchine Celibi/The Bachelor Machines*. Ed. Harald Szeemann. New York: Rizzoli.

Certeau, Michel de. 1975. "Arts of Dying/Anti-Mystical Writing." In *Le Macchine Celibi/The Bachelor Machines*. Ed. Harald Szeemann. New York: Rizzoli.

Coleridge, Samuel Taylor. 1913. *Biographia Literaria*. London: Dent.

Crichton, Michael. 1990. *Jurassic Park*. New York: Knopf.

Crookes, William. 1897. "De La Relativité des Connaissances Humaines." *Revue Scientifique* 20, no.4.vii (15 May): 609–13.

Darwin, Erasmus. 1973. *The Botanic Garden*. Menston, Yorkshire: Scolar.

Daumal, René. 1995. *You've Always Been Wrong*. Trans. Thomas Vosteen. Lincoln: University of Nebraska Press.

Davey, Frank. 1983. *Surviving the Paraphrase*. Winnipeg: Turnstone.

Dawkins, Richard. 1989. *The Selfish Gene*. New York: Oxford University Press.

Deleuze, Gilles. 1990. *The Logic of Sense*. Ed. Constantin V. Boundas. Trans. Mark Lester and Charles Stivale. New York: Columbia University Press.

———. 1997. *Essays Critical and Clinical*. Trans. Daniel W. Smith and Michael A. Greco. Minneapolis: University of Minneapolis Press.

Deleuze, Gilles, and Félix Guattari. 1983. *Anti-Oedipus: Capitalism and Schizophrenia*. Trans. Robert Hurley, Mark Seem, and Helen R. Lane. Minneapolis: University of Minnesota Press.

———. 1987. *A Thousand Plateaus: Capitalism and Schizophrenia*. Trans. Brian Massumi. Minneapolis: University of Minnesota Press.

Derrida, Jacques. 1978. *Writing and Difference*. Trans. Alan Bass. Chicago: University of Chicago Press.

———. 1984. "My Chances/*Mes Chances:* A Rendezvous with Some Epicurean Stereophonies." In *Taking Chances: Derrida, Psychoanalysis, and Literature*. Ed. Joseph H. Smith and William Kerrigan. Baltimore: Johns Hopkins University Press.

Dewdney, Christopher. 1973. *A Palaeozoic Geology of London, Ontario*. Toronto: Coach House.

———. 1975. *Fovea Centralis*. Toronto: Coach House.

———. 1980. *Alter Sublime*. Toronto: Coach House.

———. 1980–81. "Parasite Maintenance." *Open Letter: Canadian 'Pataphysics* 4, no. 6/7 (winter): 19–35.

———. 1982. *Spring Trances in the Control Emerald Night/The Cenozoic Asylum.* Berkeley, Calif.: Figures.

———. 1983. *Predators of the Adoration: Selected Poems 1972–1982.* Toronto: McClelland and Stewart.

———. 1986. *The Immaculate Perception.* Toronto: Anansi.

———. 1987. *Permugenesis: A Recombinant Text.* Toronto: Nightwood.

———. 1988. *The Radiant Inventory.* Toronto: McClelland and Stewart.

———. 1990. "Interview with Christopher Dewdney." With Lola Lemire Tostevin. *Open Letter* 7, no. 7 (spring):84–95.

———. 1991. *Concordat Proviso Ascendant.* Great Barrington, Mass.: The Figures.

Donne, John. 1985. *The Complete English Poems of John Donne.* Ed. C. A. Patrides. London: Dent.

Duchamp, Marcel. 1971. *Dialogues with Marcel Duchamp.* With Pierre Cabanne. Trans. Ron Padgett. New York: Viking Press.

Dufresne, Todd. 1993. "Derrida, Jarry, Nietzsche: Introducing a Deconstructive Pataphysics, Contra Heidegger." *Re:Post* 1 (summer): 26–33.

Eliot, T. S. 1950. *Selected Essays.* New York: Harcourt, Brace.

Fassio, F. 1961. "La Terre de 'Pataphysique." *Dossiers du Collège de Pataphysique* 16 (1 September [22 phalle 88 e.p.]): 30–31.

Feyerabend, Paul. 1978. *Against Method: Outline of an Anarchistic Theory of Knowledge.* London: Verso.

Fort, Charles. 1974. *The Complete Books of Charles Fort.* New York: Dover.

Foucault, Michel. 1973. *The Order of Things: An Archaeology of the Human Sciences.* New York: Vintage.

———. 1977. *Language, Counter-Memory, Practice: Selected Essays and Interviews.* Ed Donald F. Bouchard. Trans. Donald F. Bouchard and Sherry Simon. Ithaca, N.Y.: Cornell University Press.

Fournel, Paul. 1986. "The Theater Tree." In *Oulipo: A Primer of Potential Literature.* Ed. and trans. Warren F. Motte. Lincoln: University of Nebraska Press.

Frye, Northrop. 1971. *The Bush Garden.* Toronto: Anansi.

Genette, Gérard. 1997. *Palimpsests: Literature in the Second Degree.* Trans. Channa Newman and Claude Doubinsky. Lincoln: University of Nebraska Press.

Genosko, Gary. 1994. *Baudrillard and Signs: Signification Ablaze.* London: Routledge.

Glover, R. 1972. "A Poem on Sir Isaac Newton." In *A View of Sir Isaac Newton's Philosophy.* New York: Johnson Reprint.

Graal-Arelsky. 1988. "Egopoetry in Poetry." In *Russian Futurism through Its Manifestoes: 1912–1928.* Ed. and trans. Anna Lawton and Herbert Eagle. Ithaca, N.Y.: Cornell University Press.

Greimas, Algirdas Julien. 1987. *On Meaning: Selected Writings*. Trans. Paul J. Perron and Frank H Collins. Minneapolis: University of Minnesota.

Hale, Terry. 1995. "Introduction to *Euphorisms*." In *4 Dada Suicides: Arthur Cravan, Jacques Rigaut, Julien Torma, and Jacques Vaché*. London: Atlas.

Hallyn, Fernand. 1990. *The Poetic Structure of the World: Copernicus and Kepler*. New York: Zone.

Harraway, Donna J. 1991. *Simians, Cyborgs, and Women: The Reinvention of Nature*. London: Free Association.

Heidegger, Martin. 1977. *The Question Concerning Technology and Other Essays*. Trans. William Lovitt. New York: Harper and Row.

Hilbert, David. 1947. *The Fundamentals of Geometry*. Trans. E. J. Townsend. La Salle: Open Court.

Hjelmslev, Louis. 1969. *Prolegomena to a Theory of Language*. Trans. Francis J. Whitfield. Madison: University of Wisconsin Press.

Hofstadter, Douglas. 1979. *Gödel, Escher, Bach: An Eternal Golden Braid*. New York: Basic Books.

Hulten, Pontus. 1987. *Jean Tinguely: A Magic Stronger Than Death*. New York: Abbeville.

Huxley, Aldous. 1963. *Literature and Science*. London: Chatto and Windus.

Huxley, T. H. 1948. *Selections from the Essays*. Ed. Alburey Castell. Arlington Heights, Ill.: Harlan Davidson.

Jarry, Alfred. 1964. *The Supermale*. Trans. Ralph Gladstone and Barbara Wright. New York: New Directions.

———. 1965. *Selected Works of Alfred Jarry*. Ed. Roger Shattuck and Simon Watson Taylor. New York: Grove.

———. 1989. *Days and Nights*. Trans. Alexis Lykiard. London: Atlas.

———. 1992. *Caesar Antichrist*. Trans. Antony Melville. London: Atlas.

Jirgens, Karl. 1986. "Editorial." *Rampike: La 'Pataphysique*, 2.

Jones, William Powell. 1966. *The Rhetoric of Science: A Study of Scientific Ideas and Imagery in Eighteenth-Century English Poetry*. Berkeley: University of California Press.

Keats, John. 1959. *Selected Poems and Letters*. Ed. Douglas Bush. Boston: Houghton Mifflin.

Kelvin, Lord (Sir William Thomson). 1889. *Popular Lectures and Address*. Vol. 1. London: Macmillan.

Khlebnikov, Velimir. 1987. *Collected Works of Velimir Khlebnikov: Letters and Theoretical Writings*. Ed. Charlotte Douglas. Trans. Paul Schmidt. Cambridge: Harvard University Press.

Kristeva, Julia. 1982. *The Powers of Horror*. New York: Columbia University Press.

Kroetsch, Robert. 1989. *The Lovely Treachery of Words: Essays Selected and New*. Toronto: Oxford.

Kuhn, Thomas S. 1970. *The Structure of Scientific Revolutions.* 2d ed. Chicago: University of Chicago Press.

Lawton, Anna, and Herbert Eagle, eds. 1988. *Russian Futurism through Its Manifestoes: 1912–1928.* Trans. Anna Lawton and Herbert Eagle. Ithaca, N.Y.: Cornell University Press.

Lear, Edward. 1947. *The Complete Nonsense of Edward Lear.* Ed. Holbrook Jackson. London: Faber and Faber.

Lennon, John, and Paul McCartney. 1970. "Maxwell's Silver Hammer." *Abbey Road.* London: Apple Records.

Lescure, Jean. 1986. "Brief History of the Oulipo." In *Oulipo: A Primer of Potential Literature.* Ed. and trans. Warren F. Motte. Lincoln: University of Nebraska Press.

Lucretius. 1975. *De Rerum Natura.* Trans. W. H. D. Rouse. Cambridge: Harvard University Press.

Lyotard, Jean-François. 1984. *The Postmodern Condition: A Report on Knowledge.* Trans. Geoff Bennington and Brian Massumi. Minneapolis: University of Minnesota Press.

———. 1990. *Duchamp's TRANS/formers.* Venice: Lapis Press.

———. 1993. *Libidinal Economy.* Trans. Iain Hamilton Grant. Bloomington: Indiana University Press.

Marinetti, F. T. 1987. *Stung by Salt and War: Creative Texts of the Italian Avant-Gardist F. T. Marinetti.* Ed. Richard J. Pioli. New York: Peter Lang.

———. 1991. *Let's Murder the Moonshine: Selected Writings.* Ed. R. W. Flint. Trans. R. W. Flint and Arthur A. Coppatelli. Los Angeles: Sun and Moon.

Mathews, Harry. 1986. "Mathew's Algorithm." In *Oulipo: A Primer of Potential Literature.* Ed. and trans. Warren F. Motte. Lincoln: University of Nebraska Press.

McCaffery, Steve. 1980–81. "The F-Claim to Shape in a 'Patalogomena towards a Zero Reading (For Ihab Hassan)." *Open Letter: Canadian 'Pataphysics* 4, no. 6/7 (winter): 11–13.

———. 1981. *The Perseus Project: Paleogorgonization and the Sexual Life of Fossils.* Toronto: Institute for Creative Misunderstanding.

———. 1986. "Strata and Strategy: 'Pataphysics in the Poetry of Christopher Dewdney." In *North of Intention: Critical Writings 1973–1986.* New York: Roof. Toronto: Nightwood.

———. 1997. "Zarathustran 'Pataphysics." *Open Letter* 9, no. 7 (winter): 11–22.

McFadden, David. 1978. "The Twilight of Self-Consciousness." In *The Human Elements.* Ed. David Helwig. Ottawa: Oberon.

Motte, Warren F. 1986. "Clinamen Redux." *Comparative Literature Studies* 23, no. 4 (winter): 263–81.

Nichol, bp. 1980. *As Elected: Selected Writing.* Vancouver: Talonbooks.

———. 1980–81. "Rediscovery of the 22-Letter Alphabet: An Archaeological Report." *Open Letter: Canadian "Pataphysics* 4, no. 6/7 (winter): 41–47.

———. 1985a. "Digging Up the Pas T." In *Papers Delivered at the Symposium of Linguistic Onto-Genetics Held in Toronto, Canada.* grOnk Final Series 5 (March). Ed. Writers in Support of Alphabet Archaeology.

———. 1985b. *Zygal: A Book of Mysteries and Translations.* Toronto: Coach House.

———. 1990. *Art Facts: A Book of Contexts.* Tucson: Chax.

———. 1993. *Truth: A Book of Fictions.* Stratford, Ont.: Mercury.

Nicholson, Marjorie. 1946. *Newton Demands the Muse: Newton's 'Opticks' and the Eighteenth Century Poets.* Hamden: Archon.

Nietzsche, Friedrich. 1966. *The Birth of Tragedy* with *The Case of Wagner.* Trans. W. Kaufmann. New York: Vintage.

———. 1968. *The Will to Power.* Trans. W. Kaufmann and R. J. Hollingdale. New York: Vintage.

———. 1974. *The Gay Science.* Trans. Walter Kaufmann. New York: Vintage.

———. 1979. *Philosophy and Truth: Selections from Nietzsche's Notebooks of the Early 1870's.* Trans. Daniel Breazeale. Atlantic Highlands, N.J.: Humanities Press.

———. 1982. *Daybreak.* Trans. R. J. Hollingdale. Cambridge: Cambridge University Press.

Oulipo. 1986. *Oulipo: A Primer of Potential Literature.* Ed. and trans. Warren F. Motte. Lincoln: University of Nebraska Press.

———. 1995. *Oulipo Laboratory: Texts from the Bibliothèque Oulipienne.* Trans. Harry Mathews, Iain White, and Warren Motte Jr. London: Atlas.

———. 1998. *Oulipo Compendium.* Ed. Harry Mathews and Alastair Brotchie. London: Atlas.

Paulson, William R. 1988. *The Noise of Culture: Literary Texts in a World of Information.* Ithaca, N.Y.: Cornell University Press.

Perec, Georges. 1985. *Alphabets: cent soixante-seize onzains hétérogrammatiques.* Paris: Galilée.

———. 1986. "History of the Lipogram." In *Oulipo: A Primer of Potential Literature.* Ed and trans. Warren F. Motte. Lincoln: University of Nebraska Press.

———. 1987. *Life: A User's Manual.* Trans. David Bellos. London: Collins Harvill.

———. 1994. *A Void.* Trans. Gilbert Adair. London: Harvill.

Pickover, Clifford A. 1994. *Chaos in Wonderland: Visual Adventures in a Fractal World.* New York: St. Martin's.

Prigogine, Ilya, and Isabelle Stengers. 1984. *Order out of Chaos: Man's New Dialogue with Nature.* New York: Bantam.

Queneau, Raymond. 1950. "Quelque remarques sommaires relatives aux propriétés aérodynamiques de l'addition." *Cahiers du Collège de 'Pataphysique* 1 (6 April [15 *Clinamen* 77 e.p.]): 21–22.

———. 1961. *Cent mille milliards de poémes.* Paris: Gallimard.

———. 1986a. "Potential Literature." In *Oulipo: A Primer of Potential Literature.* Ed. and trans. Warren F. Motte. Lincoln: University of Nebraska Press.

———. 1986b. "A Story As You Like It." In *Oulipo: A Primer of Potential Literature.* Ed. and trans. Warren F. Motte. Lincoln: University of Nebraska Press.

———. 1995. "The Foundations of Literature (After David Hilbert)." In *Oulipo Laboratory: Texts from the Bibliothèque Oulipienne.* Trans. Harry Mathews, Iain White, and Warren Motte Jr. London: Atlas.

RACTER. 1984. *The Policeman's Beard Is Half Constructed.* New York: Warner Books.

Richards, I. A. 1926. *Science and Poetry.* London: Kegan Paul, Trench, Trubner, and Co.

Rossiyanski, M. 1988. "From 'Moment Philosophique.'" In *Russian Futurism through Its Manifestoes: 1912–1928.* Ed. and trans. Anna Lawton and Herbert Eagle. Ithaca, N.Y.: Cornell University Press.

Roubaud, Jacques. 1981. "Deux Principes parfois respectés par les travaux oulipiens," In *Atlas de littérature potentielle.* Paris: Gallimard.

———. 1986. "Mathematics in the Method of Raymond Queneau." In *Oulipo: A Primer of Potential Literature.* Ed. and trans. Warren F. Motte. Lincoln: University of Nebraska Press.

Russolo, Luigi. 1967. *The Art of Noise: Futurist Manifesto, 1913.* Trans. Robert Filliou. New York: Something Else.

Sandomir, I. L. 1960a. "Allocution Pronounced at the Inauguration of the Expojarrysition." *Evergreen Review* 4, no. 13 (May–June): 173.

———. 1960b. "Extract from the Prostheses (upon Ubu and the Serious)." *Evergreen Review* 4, no. 13 (May–June): 174–77.

———. 1960c. "Extract from the Testament of Dr. I. L. Sandomir." *Evergreen Review* 4, no. 13 (May–June): 178–80.

———. 1960d. "Inaugural Harangue." *Evergreen Review* 4, no. 13 (May–June): 169–73.

Schlegel, Friedrich. 1971. *Friedrich Schlegel's Lucinde and the Fragments.* Trans. Peter Firchow. Minneapolis: University of Minnesota Press.

Serres, Michel. 1975. "It Was before the (World-) Exhibition." In *Le Macchine Celibi (The Bachelor Machines).* New York: Rizzoli.

———. 1982a. *Hermes: Literature, Science, Philosophy.* Ed. Josué V. Harari and David F. Bell. Baltimore: Johns Hopkins University Press.

———. 1982b. *The Parasite.* Trans. Lawrence R. Schehr. Baltimore: Johns Hopkins University Press.

———. 1995. *Genesis.* Trans. Geneviève James and James Nielson. Ann Arbor: University of Michigan Press.

Shattuck, Roger. 1984. *The Innocent Eye.* New York: Farrar, Straus, and Giroux.

Shelley, Mary. 1985. *Frankenstein.* Ed. Maurice Hindle. London: Penguin.

Shershenevich, V. 1988. "From Green Street." In *Russian Futurism through Its Manifestoes: 1912–1928.* Ed. and trans. Anna Lawton and Herbert Eagle. Ithaca, N.Y.: Cornell University Press.

Shklovsky, Victor. 1965. "Art as Technique." In *Russian Formalist Criticism.* Trans. Lee T. Lemon and Marion J. Reis. Lincoln: University of Nebraska Press.

Snow, C. P. 1959. *The Two Cultures and the Scientific Revolution.* New York: Cambridge University Press.

Sprat, Thomas. 1958. *History of the Royal Society.* Ed. Jackson I. Cope and Harold Whitmore Jones. St. Louis: Washington University Press.

Starobinski, Jean. 1979. *Words upon Words: The Anagrams of Saussure.* Trans. Olivia Emmet. New Haven, Conn.: Yale University Press.

Stillman, Linda Klieger. 1983. *Alfred Jarry.* Boston: Twayne.

Swift, Jonathan. 1960. "A Voyage to Laputa." In *Gulliver's Travels and Other Writings.* Ed. Louis A. Landa. Boston: Houghton Mifflin.

Szeemann, Harald, ed. 1975. *Le Macchine Celibi/The Bachelor Machines.* New York: Rizzoli.

Taylor, Simon Watson. 1960. "The College of 'Pataphysics: An Apodeictic Outline." *Evergreen Review* 4, no. 13 (May–June): 150–57.

Thomas, Jean-Jacques. 1981. "README.DOC: On Oulipo." *Substance* 54:18–28.

Torma, Julien. 1995. "Julien Torma to René Daumal, Lille, 20 october, 1929." In *4 Dada Suicides: Selected Texts of Arthur Cravan, Jacques Rigaut, Julien Torma, and Jacque Vaché.* Trans. Terry Hale, Paul Lenti, Iain White, et al. London: Atlas.

Thomson, James. 1853. *Thomson's Poetical Works.* Edinburgh: Nisbet.

Toronto Research Group (TRG), eds. 1980–81. *Open Letter: Canadian 'Pataphysics* 4, no.6/7 (winter).

———. 1992. *Rational Geomancy: The Kids of the Book-Machine: The Collected Research Reports of the Toronto Research Group 1973–1982.* Ed. Steve McCaffery. Vancouver: Talonbooks.

Truhlar, Richard. 1980–81. "Toward a Constructivist Theory of Linguistic Onto-Genetics." *Open Letter: Canadian 'Pataphysics* 4, no. 6/7 (winter): 99–107.

———. 1985. *Trace-Form Imagery in Venetian Ornamental Cookery.* Toronto: Underwhich.

Turing, A. M. 1981. "Computing Machinery and Intelligence." In *The Mind's I.* Ed. Douglas R. Hofstadter and Daniel C. Dennet. New York: Bantam.

Tynyanov, Y. 1979. "About Khlebnikov." In *The Futurists, the Formalists, and the Marxist Critique.* Ed. Christopher Pike and Joe Andrew. London: Ink Links.

Vaihinger, Hans. 1966. *The Philosophy of "As If": A System of the Theoretical, Practical, and Religious Fictions of Mankind.* Trans. C. L. Ogden. New York: Barnes and Noble.

Vaneigem, Raoul. 1994. *The Revolution of Everyday Life.* Trans. Donald Nicholson-Smith. London: Left Bank Books.

Vico, Giambattista. 1984. *The New Science of Giambattista Vico.* Trans. Thomas Goddard Bergin and Max Harold Fisch. Ithaca, N.Y.: Cornell University Press.

Virilio, Paul. 1986. *Speed and Politics.* Trans. Mark Polizzotti. New York: Semiotext(e).

Wells, H. G. 1987. *The Definitive Time Machine: A Critical Edition of H. G. Wells's Scientific Romance.* Ed. Harry M. Geduld. Bloomington: University of Indiana Press.

Wershler-Henry, Darren. 1994. "Canadian 'Pataphysics: Geognostic Interrogations of a Distant Somewhere." In *Semiotext(e) Canadas.* New York: Semiotext(e).

Weschler, Lawrence. 1995. *Mr. Wilson's Cabinet of Wonder.* New York: Pantheon.

Wordsworth, William. 1965. *Selected Poems and Prefaces.* Ed. Jack Stillinger. Boston: Houghton Mifflin.

Writers in Support of Alphabet Archaeology, eds. 1985. *Papers Delivered at the Symposium of Linguistic Onto-Genetics Held in Toronto, Canada.* grOnk Final Series 5 (March).

Wurstwagen, Kurt. 1980–81. "Piccu-Carlu: The Muskoka-Maya Connection." *Open Letter: Canadian 'Pataphysics* 4, no. 6/7 (winter): 144–54.

Zukav, Gary. 1979. *The Dancing Wu Li Masters: An Overview of the New Physics.* New York: Morrow.

Index

Thomson, James, 20, 104n, 105n
Tinguely, Jean, 48, 50, 109n, 111n
Tlön, Uqbar, Orbis Tertius, 7, 10, 26, 103n
Torma, Julien, 28, 34
Toronto Research Group (TRG), 82–84, 86, 96, 97, 114n, 115n
Tracy, Destutt de, 72
Traumwelt, 25, 31, 37, 57, 67, 94
Truhlar, Richard, 85, 86, 114n
Turing, A. M., 114n
Tynyanov, Y., 58, 59

Ubu Roi, 13, 24, 27, 28, 36, 43, 48, 97, 104n, 109n

Vaihinger, Hans, 8, 25
Vaneigem, Raoul, 5, 100, 103n, 117n

velocità, la (speed), 47, 48, 54, 59–62
Vico, Giambattista, 18, 104n
Victory of Samothrace, 48
Virilio, Paul, 59, 111n

Wells, H. G., 60
Wershler-Henry, Darren, 81, 82, 86, 97
Weschler, Lawrence, 3, 103n
Wilson, David, 3, 4
Wordsworth, William, 21, 22, 105n
Writers in Support of Alphabet Archaeology, 85, 90, 115n
Wunderkammern, 3, 5, 35
Wurstwagen, Kurt, 86, 87

Zarathustra, 33, 36, 44
Zukav, Gary, 42

Christian Bök is a Social Sciences and Humanities Research Council Fellow affiliated with the Poetics Program at SUNY-Buffalo. Bök is the author of *Crystallography: Book I of Information Theory,* a nominee for the Gerald Lampert Memorial Award given for best poetic debut. He has published numerous articles on Canadian avant-garde poetry in *Open Letter, Canadian Literature,* and *Studies in Canadian Literature,* and his own experimental poetry has been frequently anthologized, appearing most recently in *Imagining Language.*